New Library of Pastoral Care
GENERAL EDITOR: DEREK BLOWS

Make or Break

New Library of Pastoral Care
GENERAL EDITOR: DEREK BLOWS

―――

MAKE OR BREAK

An Introduction to Marriage Counselling

―――

Jack Dominian

First published 1984
Third impression 1987
SPCK
Holy Trinity Church
Marylebone Road
London NW1 4DU

Acknowledgement
Biblical quotations are from the Jerusalem Bible, and are
reproduced by permission of Darton, Longman & Todd.

British Library Cataloguing in Publication Data
Dominian, Jack
   Make or break. — (New library of pastoral care)
   1. Marriage counselling
   1. Title   II. Series
   362.8′286   HQ10

ISBN 0 281 04075 3

Filmset by Pioneer
Printed and bound in Great Britain by
Anchor Brendon Limited, Tiptree, Essex

Contents

Foreword

The *New Library of Pastoral Care* has been planned to meet the needs of those people concerned with pastoral care, whether clergy or lay, who seek to improve their knowledge and skills in this field. Equally, it is hoped that it may prove useful to those secular helpers who may wish to understand the role of the pastor.

Pastoral care in every age has drawn from contemporary secular knowledge to inform its understanding of man and his various needs and of the ways in which these needs might be met. Today it is perhaps the secular helping professions of social work, counselling and psychotherapy, and community development which have particular contributions to make to the pastor in his work. Such knowledge does not stand still, and a pastor would have a struggle to keep up with the endless tide of new developments which pour out from these and other disciplines, and to sort out which ideas and practices might be relevant to his particular pastoral needs. Among present-day ideas, for instance, of particular value might be an understanding of the social context of the pastoral task, the dynamics of the helping relationship, the attitudes and skills as well as factual knowledge which might make for effective pastoral intervention, and perhaps most significant of all, the study of particular cases, whether through verbatim reports of interviews or general case presentation. The discovery of ways of learning from what one is doing is becoming increasingly important.

There is always a danger that a pastor who drinks deeply at the well of a secular discipline may lose his grasp of his own pastoral identity and become 'just another' social worker or counsellor. It in no way detracts from the value of these professions to assert that the role and task of the pastor are quite unique among the helping professions and deserve to be clarified and strengthened rather than weakened. The theological commitment of the pastor and the appropriate use of his role will be a recurrent theme of the series. At the same time the pastor cannot afford to work in a vacuum. He needs to be able to communicate and co-operate with those helpers in other disciplines whose work may overlap, without loss of his own unique role. This in turn will mean being able to communicate with them through some understanding of their concepts and language.

Finally, there is a rich variety of styles and approaches in pastoral work within the various religious traditions. No attempt will be made to secure a uniform approach. The Library will contain the variety, and even perhaps occasional eccentricity, which such a title suggests. Some books will be more specifically theological and others more concerned with particular areas of need or practice. It is hoped that all of them will have a usefulness that will reach right across the boundaries of religious denomination.

DEREK BLOWS
Series Editor

Preface

———

At a time when divorce is at an unprecedentedly high level the number of couples who are seeking help for their marital problems is also on the increase. Help is sought from ministers and their assistants, teachers, social workers, doctors and ultimately any one of us who form the intimate family circle of the spouses. It is important in these circumstances that as many people as possible are informed about the nature of marital difficulties, how they arise and the way they are presented. The emphasis of this book is on understanding these problems in the light of contemporary changes in marriage.

It is vital that the person who responds to a plea for help, who in fact gives first aid, does this sensitively and within a framework that will be immediately helpful. In other words the helper should be able to throw enough light on the problem to enable its nature to be understood. So often people give advice which springs from their own experience which is irrelevant to the marital issues with which they are presented. This book aims to provide a minimum outline with which a problem can be listened to and recognized.

Having done this, the helper may wish to proceed to some elementary marriage counselling or to send the person to one of the recognized marriage counselling bodies. So often however people do not want to sever the useful connection they have made and they want to continue coming back. This book tries to assist with the elementary principles of counselling, so that this can be undertaken if needed. Although it is primarily addressed to the clergy, anyone in a caring role should find it helpful. But it must be stressed that if marriage counselling is to become a regular part of a situation then proper training is needed. No claim is made that this text is sufficient in itself to produce the complete marriage counsellor.

Nevertheless anyone who has already some counselling or

psychotherapy experience in other fields will find the book useful in introducing them to the area of marriage. Trained marriage counsellors and those in training may find a new approach which will complement other sources. The list of references for further reading is meant to extend the depth of interest for those who want further specialized knowledge. Throughout the text the counsellor is designated as 'he', but this stands for both sexes, and the masculine is used without any bias as a way of avoiding tedious repetition.

This book reflects not only my special interest and approach to marital problems but it also derives much strength from the continuous research and work carried out at the Marital Research Centre, Central Middlesex Hospital, London.

Finally, although my background is Christian and this is reflected in the writing, the contents of the book can be used by anyone with any faith or set of values. Its basic concern is the integrity of love in marriage which is of universal concern.

JACK DOMINIAN
May 1983

PART ONE

ONE

The Role of The Pastor

Marriage counselling challenges many of the traditional and familiar attitudes of clergy of all denominations. In general the role of the clergy in the Christian community is to lead, to give an example, to direct with authority, to sharpen the moral quest of Christians. Many ministers wonder how their authoritative approach can combine with the non-directive one of counselling. They may find themselves in difficult situations, reconciling the counsel of perfection in keeping a marriage alive with the stark reality that it is dead. They will recognize that, in dealing with the marriages of others, feelings about their own marriage will be stirred up. These topics cannot be examined exhaustively, but suggestions will be made about the specific approach of counselling.

Authority and conscience

The married often go to the clergy for guidance regarding decision-making in their marital difficulties. Should a spouse continue in a difficult or even impossible marriage? How do they come to terms with an unfaithful partner? Does one put the children before one's own interests? These and similar questions are presented. The minister listens and he is often expected to deliver the traditional Christian reply. Christian marriage is meant to be permanent. Adultery should be forgiven. Children need both parents. These answers are expected and given without any hesitation. The minister sees himself as an upholder of the truth, and his task is to convince those in doubt to persist in the righteous path, however difficult it is.

Unfortunately such a traditional exchange between presenting the problem and receiving the expected reply is not always very productive. Those who inquire know the answer in advance and the response, however kindly given, does not often mobilize greater motivation to persevere. The inquirer often knows what the Christian teaching is and, if real ignorance exists, this can soon be remedied. But the clergyman has a much more challenging task. He has to listen at length and explain clearly the Christian teaching, but it is even more important that he tries to appreciate the difficulties which the man or woman in front of him has, which prevents them from carrying out the dictates of their conscience.

This is often more complex and demanding. The minister needs to tease out what is the state of the marriage, what the husband or wife feels about the situation, and finally the conversation should conclude with the inquirer having to use his or her moral resources to decide what to do. So many people go to a priest and enact an prearranged drama. They put a question, the answers to which they know perfectly well. Having heard it, they go away with the feeling that the church lays down the law but cannot help. Thousands of clergy co-operate with this aridity by giving the official reply, kindly or curtly, and, one way or another, close the discussion.

This book aims to encourage a conversation that does not begin and end with authoritative pronouncements that are already known. An informed priest facilitates a conversation that examines the marriage in such a way, that already, during the discussion, the married person begins to appreciate that the responsibility for the right decision is in his/her hands. When he has been helped to examine his marriage as a relationship of love and also the resources of the couple to translate this commitment to a reality, then, if there is any possibility of doing so, clearly Christian teaching requires this. But this decision should emerge from the insights of the dialogue and not from the authority of the clergyman. In so far as the latter is expected to uphold the law and the ideal, he is not really giving anything new. In so far as he has helped those in trouble to see for themselves what the situation is, and in this way has encouraged them to increase their motivation to overcome the difficulties, then he has stimulated the *active* co-operation of the person concerned.

Furthermore, having raised the level of motivation to overcome the difficulties, he has also sharpened the conscience of the inquirer who is now no longer a passive receiver of advice but an active ally in a moral quest.

Sometimes however the conclusion is negative. An examination of the total situation of marriage in its various dimensions reveals that there is no substance left. So often the person who inquires wants to be told what to do. The priest is seen as a figure of authority who instructs. But the instruction will fall on deaf ears if there is no real understanding of what the issues are. The priest needs to help married people look very carefully at their married state and, after examining the social, emotional, sexual, intellectual and spiritual dimensions, help a couple look at what is present and what can be generated afresh. If the answer is nil, then it is the couple or the individual who has to make the decision. It is his/her conscience that has to operate. Roman Catholics are still having to do this with regard to contraception and abortion. The priest's role is to listen, explain the church's teaching, but it is the couple who have to take the decision. The situation is similar in matters of permanency, separation or divorce. An informed pastor's task is to help a couple to see for themselves what is possible in their marriage and encourage them to take their considered decision. Whatever conclusion is reached, it is vital that the couple feel they can return to the pastor and stay within the life of the church. An authoritative reply is often interpreted that, if it is disobeyed, then this also spells out the rejection from the life of the church; whereas in fact the church exists as much for sinners as for the righteous.

Authority and nourishing

The pastor, who is clear about Christian teaching but encourages the couple to use their consciences in making their decision, thus remains available to nourish this couple in whatever state they find themselves. If they decide to persist with their marriage, they can come back to him for further discussion or he can refer them for marriage counselling. Whatever step is taken he remains their friend, offering sustained encouragement during their difficulties. He is no longer seen as a figure of authority who judges their progress but as someone who shares their agony and transforms it into a Christian pilgrimage. So often the clergy are seen as figures who have to maintain the sanctity of marriage as a principle from afar. If the parish and its members gradually appreciates that there are a dozen marriages which are being helped directly or indirectly, then the combination of sharing and safeguarding ideals becomes an active force of encouragement.

But the nourishing is also spiritual. So many people who go to a priest with a problem, any problem, are given an authoritative answer and then told to pray or go to the sacraments. This is the type of approach that often alienates. When someone is in difficulty, they need to feel that the pain and suffering they are experiencing is recognized and appreciated. The advice to pray, sound as it is, often appears as a way of getting rid of the person. When the specific nature of the marital difficulty is recognized, then the praying and the turning to God is intimately related to the nature of the problem and both pastor and couple are together turning to God for help. The spiritual nourishing is tailored to the unfolding progress of the problem, and the most urgent need of any Christian, namely to see the link between human reality and divine response, is much more likely to be recognized and appreciated.

Furthermore, this spiritual nourishing is not only addressed to the couple in question. Preaching on marriage should leave the ethereal and often idealistic tone and descend to the daily experience of married couples, who are then helped to see that what is happening in their everyday life is appreciated by the clergy. A suitable liturgy can also be organized to reflect the reality of contemporary marriage.

Feelings

In the course of listening to a marital problem, the feelings of both the couple and that of the pastor are mobilized. Everyone in a position of authority can use his position to instruct and to advise, and in this way he keeps his own feelings out of the exchange. In counselling or even listening to a marriage problem, feelings are aroused in the pastor. If married, he may see in the problem presented his own marital difficulties.

He may have his own fears, anxieties, anger aroused and his own sensitivities heightened. If he is afraid of feelings, his own and those of the couple, he will try to avoid them by appealing to reason and Christian morality, but feelings are a large part of marital conflict.

By recognizing and allowing his own feelings to surface, the pastor will have a much better appreciation of what he is listening to. In acknowledging his own feelings, he will note whether his responses are biased towards either spouse and simultaneously he will be able to stay close to the couple rather than trying to divert them to rational, practical or moral decisions. If spouses are hurt, it is no good urging forgiveness until the pain has been allayed. If the ideal of a spouse has been shattered by the other's infidelity, time is needed to reconstruct a new and more authentic image of the person they are married to. If a partner feels cheated, betrayed and let down, then allowance has to be made for the anger elicited.

Anger, which is the converse side of love, is often present when a couple in conflict are talking to each other in front of the pastor. They row, exchange unpleasant remarks, shout, scream and even come to blows. Anyone who is not accustomed to seeing this happen feels extremely uncomfortable in its presence. Clergy, who feel that peace, serenity and love should be the manifestations of marriage, may find the active exchange of conflict in their presence very disturbing. Sometimes it stirs up their own highly suppressed anger and they feel that they have to bring the exchange to a speedy conclusion at any price. But this is not necessarily what is right. A couple may find that they can only express their anger to each other in front of the pastor, and they need his presence to release pent-up feelings. A pastor has to have the confidence to let the angry exchange occur and to remind the couple that Christ himself experienced and expressed anger. Clearly the task of counselling is to go beyond anger and to understand the reasons underlying such feelings.

In the process of listening and/or counselling, the pastor may find either that he too is getting angry with one or both partners or that he is taking an immense dislike to one or both. This will be highly disturbing. Such negativity has to be recognized, and at the appropriate moment disclosed, if the counselling is to be helped. Thus he can say that the repeated accusations, criticisms, sarcasms, humiliation of one partner is clearly evoking anger in the other and that he too is feeling angry at what he is seeing. Sometimes the repeated angry responses of one spouse are hiding pain, fear or insecurity, and there is a need to recognize this. Anger expresses many underlying feelings, and by allowing its ventilation the couple move forward in understanding their interaction, and the pastor is recognized as being a sensitive, empathetic person instead of being aloof and uninvolved. So that peace at any price is not the answer in marriage or counselling.

Patterns of marriage

Couples bring to a pastor a whole variety of styles of marriage. They range from the traditional patterns, in which the husband is the head of the family and the provider and the wife is the mother and homemaker, to actual reversal of roles. In a reverse marriage role, it is the husband who stays at home and looks after the children and the wife who goes out and works. Within these wide parameters all sorts of variations exist. In some marriages the husband is the figure of authority, in others it is the wife who takes command. There are relationships in which the time spent together by the couple is minimal and there are partners who are inseparable. Some couples may make love nightly and continue to have intercourse regularly in their sixties and seventies and others come together sexually at infrequent intervals.

Listening to such a wide spectrum of patterns, the minister may be astonished at what he hears. Sometimes very little holds a marriage together, and on other occasions a great deal is needed by one partner. His task is not to pass judgement on the variety and quality of the married life he is listening to. The pattern of an individual marriage may vary enormously from his own or what he considers normal. We are living at a time of rapid change. His task is not to provide a primer for the ideal marriage but to facilitate the meeting of the minimum needs of any couple who come to him for help.

The pastor's spiritual task is to help the couple realize that the Christian faith is about transforming the ordinary, whatever it is, into the extraordinary which is saturated with love. Where genuine love is, there God exists. His task is to indicate that the everyday experience of the couple, however unusual, is the stuff out of which their sanctity is made. Whilst offering ideals, he has to recognize that most couples' marriage is a struggle and that God is present in its midst. Christianity aims at sanctity but most of its adherents are already martyrs. There is much martyrdom in difficult marriages, and it is this which has to be recognized, and focused upon, and hope given to the couple.

The pastor's marriage

With the exception of Roman Catholic clergy, many readers of this book will be married themselves. The marriage of the vicar is something which can create tensions for him, his wife, the children and the parish. Everyone in the pastor's family may be conscious that their marriage has to be seen as a good one and, if possible, an ideal one. This may have difficulties for both the pastor and his wife, and increasingly we have become aware of the tensions in the marriages of clergy. This book is not specifically about clergy marriages. Inevitably, however, if a pastor is listening to marital problems, he may reflect on his own marriage and its own difficulties.

If he is sensitive and aware, he will appreciate that the problems he hears are not all that dissimilar from the difficulties he has to overcome in his own life. In the field of psychiatry where I work, many consider that psychiatrists, psychiatric nurses, psychologists and social workers either have no problems or that they overcome them. The truth is that the ranks of these workers are full of sensitive, vulnerable people whose formal training in no way eliminates their frailties or problems. Some of them are indeed fortunate in overcoming their individual difficulties, and a combination of learning skills, coupled with their own healed selves, makes them remarkable healers. Others have not managed to overcome their difficulties, or they remain blind to them with no insight and, despite their professional skills, they are limited in the help they can offer.

The same applies to the clergy. If they can overcome their

own sensitivities, then their integrated, whole selves, coupled with their commitment to Christ, makes them remarkable witnesses. But the clergy need to have continuous insight into themselves and must be prepared to share their own lives with those they are helping, to the extent that such sharing and disclosure is useful. They must be also constantly ready to look at their own marriage and see their own contribution to their loving relationship with their spouse and children.

A pastor must remain open to his human frailty and to the limitations in his own marriage to appreciate the same features in others. He must be conscious of his own efforts to love his own family and recognize how difficult that is, in order to recognize and appreciate the efforts of those he is counselling. A living continuity between his own marriage and those of others will make him sensitive to obstacles and difficulties and to the possibilities of sustaining, healing and growth. He will not offer and preach ideals which are unrealistic, and yet he will go on offering ideals as the goal for his own family and for the others. His marriage will not have to be either 'perfect' or 'ideal' but an ordinary one struggling to transform ordinary life into something extraordinary through love which reflects God's presence. When he, his wife or the children are in difficulties, he does not have to hide this fact from himself or from others. The Christian community is not fooled with pretence or unobtainable standards. It is impressed and moved by a shared and struggling effort which the pastor's marriage is facing, along with all the marriages of the parish.

The Roman Catholic priest

There is no doubt that marriage counselling has both advantages and disadvantages for the Roman Catholic priest. He can be more detached and therefore perhaps a better counsellor, but he may be also aloof and really unaware of the inner world of marriage. He, too, has to listen and feel and allow the couple to communicate their feelings to him. His ultimate capacity to help depends on his ability to respond and share in the world of feelings and to allow his humanity to reach that of his married parishioners.

He may be afraid that, not being married himself, he may

not understand married problems or, in the absence of appreciating marital difficulties, he may simply lay down the teaching of his church. Provided he is prepared to listen in an informed and caring way, he will come to appreciate many of the marital difficulties of the couple and be both explicit about Christian teaching on the one hand and pastorally compassionate and caring on the other. Whilst always trying to deepen the faith of his flock, ultimately he has to help them to reach their moral decisions freely in their own conscience.

A marital problem

By way of concluding this chapter I have put together an account of a marriage whose various parts are all geniune but are derived from different marriages. No solutions are given but the account is typical of some of the nightmares that have to be faced.

The couple had been married for thirteen years and had two young children, aged 10 and 8. He is 37 and she 33. He has his own business and has fallen in love with another married woman who has three children. Both couples know each other and were friends. The other woman has left her husband, is living on her own with the three children and is waiting for the decision of the man who has sought help. He has left his wife twice, has gone to live with the woman in question but on both occasions returned home.

He is a Christian with strong convictions, who feels deeply that it is wrong to leave his wife, but he feels nothing for her except compassion. He does not want to hurt her and he loves his children dearly. He cannot make up his mind what to do.

His own marriage had virtually ceased after the birth of their first child. Ever since the birth of this baby, his wife had been depressed on and off and their life had drifted apart although she still loved him very much. She had made an occasional act of love as a result of which the second child was born, but there had been no sex since the second child was born eight years ago. They did little together, and he plunged himself into work in which he was very successful. Now he recognized that the other woman meant everything to him, that he did not love his wife nor was he likely to, but he did not want to hurt her and he found separating from his children well nigh impossible.

His religious upbringing made him feel totally irresponsible at the thought of leaving his wife, but he could not love her and, although she demanded very little from him, he knew that his feelings for her were those of a brother to a sister. He could not be a husband to her and yet he could not leave although he had tried twice. His friend was getting impatient and he had a sense of impending doom that, if he did not do something soon, he would lose her. What was he to do?

An interview with his wife confirmed their non-existent sexual or emotional life and her considerable dependence on him. In fact, she said she did not mind if he had affairs provided he did not leave home. In a combined interview they talked about their childhoods, both of which were disturbed, and, in a highly emotional exchange, she pleaded at one moment for him to stay, angrily told him to go the next, then burst into tears whilst he went over to her to soothe and calm her down.

His vicar had told him that the Christian teaching was indissolubility and under no circumstances could he leave home. The problem was getting him down, he could not sleep. He had to take tablets from his doctor to calm him down, and by now thoughts of suicide were beginning to cross his mind. If he left, his wife might have a breakdown as she struggled to cope on her own. If he stayed, he could not be a husband to her and he was running the risk of losing the woman he loved. The risk of losing his children was intolerable and yet the thought of staying was reducing him to a wreck.

Faced with this couple, and in particular with this husband, what should be done? What could be done? How could the problem be tackled?

TWO

Marital Breakdown

Marital misunderstanding, conflict, stress, breakdown and divorce are not new phenomena. They can be traced as far back as there are historical records of the family. They reflect on the one hand the difficulties of maintaining harmonious accord in such an intimate relationship and on the other the depth of human yearning for stability, fidelity and love. The anger of betrayal of these hopes is intense, and the Old Testament gives us an example of the hurt husband in the marriage of Hosea. The intimate link between the love of husband and wife and that of Yahweh and his people is portrayed in the language chosen. The injured husband speaks about the misdeeds of his wife, her punishment and the ultimate reconciliation with the forgiven spouse. The same language is used to portray Yahweh's relationship with Israel in the symbolism of a husband-wife relationship. Here is the husband (Yahweh) speaking to his children about their mother (Israel):

> Denounce your mother, denounce her
> for she is not my wife
> nor am I her husband.
> Let her rid her face of her whoring,
> and her breasts of her adultery,
> or else I will strip her naked,
> expose her as on the day she was born;

HOSEA 2.4—5 (2—3)

Many partners who are unfaithful see for the time being all the advantages their lover has over their spouse. In this case Hosea's wife claims that it is her lovers who give her bread, water, wool, flax, oil and drink. The husband is indignant, as so many spouses are, at such accusations. He insists that he had been a good provider. He is so angry at the injustice of the situation that he plans to punish his wife:

> That is why, when the time comes, I mean to withdraw my corn and my wine, when the season for it comes.
> I will retrieve my wool, my flax,
> that were intended to cover her nakedness;
> so will I display her shame before her lovers' eyes
> and no one shall rescue her from my power.
>
> HOSEA 2.11 — 12 (9 — 10)

Faced with such an intense angry response, the wife has second thoughts:

> Then she will say, 'I will go back to my first husband,
> I was happier then than I am today'. HOSEA 2.9 (7)

Instead of remaining aggrieved and unmoved the husband (Yahweh) plans the reconciliation:

> That is why I am going to lure her
> and lead her out into the wilderness
> and speak to her heart.
> I am going to give her back her vineyards,
> and make the Valley of Achor a gateway of hope.
> There she will respond to me as she did when she
>   was young,
> as she did when she came out of the land of Egypt.
>
> When that day comes—it is Yahweh who speaks—
> she will call me, 'My husband',
> no longer will she call me, 'My Baal'.
>
> HOSEA 2.16 — 18 (14 — 16)

When the day of reconciliation arrives he anticipates a renewed relationship of faithfulness and love.

> When that day comes I will make a treaty on her behalf
>   with the wild animals,
> with the birds of heaven and the creeping things of the
>   earth;
> I will break bow, sword and battle in the country,
> and make her sleep secure.
> I will betroth you to myself for ever,
> betroth you with integrity and justice,

with tenderness and love;
I will betroth you to myself with faithfulness,
and you will come to know Yahweh.

HOSEA 2.20−2 (18−20)

Here is a situation where human love has gone astray but instead of leading to separation and divorce the husband aims at forgiveness and reconciliation. This human pattern is in fact a replica of how God relates to his people. They are constantly led astray by this world and he constantly forgives and reconciles in love. This basic desire for forgiveness and reconciliation confirms the revealed intention of the creator that marriage should be a permanent relationship of love lived in integrity and faithfulness, a truth of the Old Testament confirmed by Christ. Despite this ideal, divorce was permitted in Jewish law, even though reluctantly. The advent of Christianity introduced a much stricter view on divorce in the West, in contrast to the East, which has persisted to this day and is only currently being reconsidered.

It should be noted that this view of marriage, as an enduring relationship of love, is not a matter of mere law. In the Judaeo-Christian tradition it reflects a firm belief that it is a revelation which accords most accurately with the appropriate conditions for realizing the full human potential of the couple and their children. It is not an arbitrary decision made by Christians but a profoundly held conviction of both Jews and Christians that God's image is most fully reflected in a man-woman relationship which is permanent, exclusive and faithful.

This view was expressed in practice by a juridical structure in which matrimonial matters were handled by ecclesiastical courts. This practice goes back to the Middle Ages and came to an end in this country in 1857 when ecclesiastical courts were abolished and a new secular structure, the Court for Divorce and Matrimonial Causes, was set up. This court had the power to effect separation and divorce. Thus the granting of divorce by the secular arm of society began. A number of Matrimonial Acts followed that of 1857, all of which have facilitated dissolution. The last one came into operation in 1971 and brought in the revolutionary concept that a divorce should be granted on the grounds of irretrievable breakdown of marriage, even though the concept of irretrievable breakdown was assessed largely on the familiar grounds of desertion, cruelty and adultery.

The incidence of divorce has increased steadily throughout the last hundred years in England and Wales, particularly since the passage of new legislation extending the grounds for dissolution, and after the two world wars. Up to twenty years ago figures for divorce fluctuated. In the nineteenth century the numbers were of the order of 400 annually. From the turn of the century until the First World War the figures rose to about 600 yearly. There was a steady increase after the 1920s and in the following two decades the figures rose to between 3,000 and 7,000 a year. There was another jump after the Second World War to a peak of 58,000 divorces in 1947, a figure which steadily dropped to 22,000 in 1958. Since then there has been a dramatic rise as Table 1 shows.

Table 1

Year	Number of dissolutions in England and Wales	Scotland	Northern Ireland
1961	25,000	2,000	100
1966	39,000	4,000	100
1971	74,000	5,000	300
1972	119,000	6,000	400
1973	106,000	7,000	400
1974	115,000	7,000	400
1975	120,000	8,000	400
1976	126,000	9,000	400
1977	129,000	9,000	600
1978	143,000	8,000	600
1979	138,000	8,000	800
1980	148,000	9,000	900
1981	146,000		

(Source: *Social Trends,* No.12 (HMSO 1982).

It can be easily seen that the last twenty years have seen an unprecedented increase in divorce. When the figures for the United Kingdom are added up, some 158,000 divorces were granted in 1980. Since the average number of children under the age of 16 is 1.12 per divorcing couple, approximately 500,000 men, women and children are affected by divorce each year. When we compare the number involved in any other social problem including unemployment, then marital breakdown clearly emerges as the single most important social upheaval of our age; it is currently estimated to involve one in every three marriages.

Single-parent family

One of the most significant consequences of divorce is the number of families that are left with a single parent. The number involved was first estimated in 1971 as being 620,000 families. By 1976 the figure had increased to 750,000 and it is estimated that in 1980 there were 920,000 such families caring for one and a half million children. About one in eight families is headed by a lone parent, most of whom are mothers.

Lone parents face many difficulties. If they work, they have the combined responsibility of working, looking after their homes and children. Fatigue and social isolation are frequent. If they are not working, they face economic difficulties and have to rely on supplementary benefits. Separated and divorced women often have great difficulty in obtaining the maintenance awarded to them by the courts and have to rely on social security.

Thus the social situation of many single parents, particularly mothers, is most unsatisfactory, and this is reflected in the life of the children who not only miss the departed parent, often their father, but may have to live with an unhappy, depressed, irritable and tired mother.

Impact of marital breakdown

The impact of marital breakdown can be divided between the effect on the spouses and that on the children.

As far as the partners are concerned, research has shown

that during the period of the final stages of the marriage and the early months of the separation, the health of the husband and wife, particularly the latter, deteriorates. There is a rise in physical symptoms such as disturbed sleep, tiredness, loss of appetite and weight, increase in illness and even death. Spouses also suffer enormously from increased anxiety and depression, which in some instances escalates to suicide attempts and even suicide. In addition there is an increase in smoking, drinking and car accidents. These all arise from the stress of marital breakdown and the actual grief reaction resulting from the loss of the spouse. In some marriages, the departing spouse leaves a totally disconsolate partner who may be unable to adapt to the shock for months or even years.

Divorce is a severe loss, particularly if the marriage has been in existence for some years. As in every case of loss, those who are especially afflicted are those men and women who are by nature shy and lonely people, having few relations or friends available to them. Those people have relied heavily on their partner for their social and emotional support, and when their spouse leaves, they are left desolate and alone to cope with their life. Such individuals are highly vulnerable and need as much support as they can receive to negotiate this crisis in their life. In general the period between the departure of the partner and the establishment of an alternative support relationship is a highly vulnerable one in which there is a high suicide rate, warning us that those whose marriage breaks up need maximum support at the time of their separation and until they have reconstituted their life.

The impact of divorce on children is a hotly debated topic. In the absence of detailed and longitudinal studies there is much speculation about the adverse effects. An important study from the United States which followed children up to five years after divorce found that the outcome depended on several factors. A good outcome was associated with a continuing, loving and reliable relationship with the departed parent, mainly the father, the presence of a reliable and available mother who continues the role of parenting, the elimination of conflict, bitterness and persistent bickering of the divorced parents and the resources of the child socially and psychologically. A bad outcome was related to negative factors in all these instances and the authors record that at the five years stage, a third of the children were still unhappy. The more distressed children tend to show deterioration in their work at school, become emotionally upset, often depressed and a proportion develop disturbed behaviour and delinquency.

An even more important question is the long-term impact on divorced children in relation to their own future marriages. Again evidence is conflicting. There are research data that suggest a link between childhood and adult divorce. Other evidence does not confirm this. Even if marriage is not imperilled by childhood divorce experience, there is plenty of evidence to suggest that family break-up is a stress factor and that there is a high incidence of divorce in the childhood of those who later show neuroticism, alcoholism, delinquency, crime, sexual problems, personality disorders, violent behaviour and some aspects of psychiatric illness.

At the beginning of this chapter it was stressed that Christian strictures against divorce were not arbitrary rules and regulations, but reflected the deep belief that marital stability safeguarded the best interests of spouses and children to develop as human beings. It can be seen from this brief review of the adversity associated with divorce that modern research evidence amply confirms the evil of marital breakdown. This is not an evil which the partners deliberately bring about through their badness. Rather it is an evil that arises from the various deficits and negative interactions over which the majority of the married have little control or understanding. The divorced are often overwhelmed by circumstances beyond their control, although much can be done to avoid the final irretrievable breakdown and this book will be concerned with relating research findings to prevention.

One such research finding is the timing of marital breakdown. Such knowledge allows support to be given at the time of maximum vulnerability.

Timing of marital breakdown

Statistics show that nearly half of all divorces occur in the first nine years of marriage. In practice there is a gap of some three years on average between separation and divorce. Thus the critical period for marriage is earlier, in the first five or six years. Two studies have shown that between 35—40 per cent of divorces are of couples who have separated before their fifth wedding anniversary. All this indicates that the early years of marriage are crucial for its stability, a fact which is not widely appreciated. Marital difficulties which lead to divorce appear very early in marriage, some 50 per cent by the second year. Moreover, wives recognize and appreciate these difficulties much earlier than husbands. Furthermore, even when marriage ends in divorce twenty years or more after its inception, for half of these couples serious marital problems occurred in the first five years of marriage.

There is another peak of divorce after some twenty years or more, a time which coincides with the departure of children. But this peak does not offer as many opportunities for prevention as the early years.

Second marriages

Divorcees often remarry. Age is obviously important, particularly for women whose chances for remarriage diminish later in life. But for both sexes, some 80 per cent of all those who divorce under the age of 30 will remarry. It used to be thought that remarriages were more stable than first marriages. This is not the case and the rate of divorce for second marriages is increasing. Although more research and data are needed, there is some indication that divorce in second marriages is higher than in the first. So that second marriages need as much protection as first ones.

Summary

Marriages have always been vulnerable and divorce has been one solution to intolerable situations. This solution was present in the Old Testament but the ideal in the Judaeo-Christian tradition has always been indissolubility. This ideal was preserved until the last twenty years, during which time divorce has risen sharply. Research on divorce shows it has extensive and severe effects on the couple and the children, and that the factors which contribute to it appear early in marriage. Thus whilst support for marriage is needed throughout its duration, the early years, which are particularly vulnerable, require special attention.

Further reading

Recent Contributions of Christian Attitudes to Marriage and Divorce:

Marriage and the Church's Task. Church Information Office, 1978.
Pope John Paul II, *Familiaris Consortio.* Catholic Truth Society, 1981.
Kevin J. Kelly, *Divorce and Second Marriage.* Collins, 1982.

Impact of Marital Breakdown
J. Dominian, *Marital Pathology.* Darton, Longman and Todd, 1980.

THREE

The Social Factors

The most urgent question facing us is to try to understand the reasons for the massive increase in divorce, which incidentally affects the whole of Western society. Is it a transient phenomenon or does it reflect something deeper and of a more permanent nature? This is the question that will be explored in this and the two subsequent chapters.

In this chapter the social elements related to marriage are first considered. Marriage has always reflected the interaction between social and psychological factors. Social factors dictate social expectations. To what extent is a society committed to marriage? Who controls it? For example, in the past the arrangement of marriage was in the hands of the parents and elders of a community, and young people were brought together largely independently of their wishes. In Western society this structure has gradually changed to the point where the young people control their choice almost entirely. Some countries like India still have arranged marriages. Given that marriages are organized by the young, the pattern of courtship, living together prior to marriage and premarital sexual activity are all governed by changing social mores. Age at marriage, the respective roles of partners, the timing and size of the family are also socially conditioned.

All these patterns of social conduct ultimately lead to the social norms which govern the behaviour of the couple. But behaviour is not solely controlled by social factors. The personality of the individuals and their psychological make-up contribute vitally and also lead to psychological expectations. Thus ultimately the intimate behaviour of marriage is governed by social factors on the one hand and psychological factors on the other. As we shall see, both have altered substantially, and contemporary marriage has to cope with major changes for which there is no adequate education, preparation or support.

There are broadly two categories of social factors which impinge on marriage. The first consists of major changes in the social behaviour of men and women, particularly the latter. The second is the contribution of individual social factors which research has isolated and shown to be linked with marital breakdown.

Major social changes

A number of the major changes affect the position of women and therefore indirectly influence the man-woman relationship. The first contribution is the women's emancipation movement. It is a movement which began some two hundred years ago but has rapidly accelerated this century and particularly in the last twenty years. Women's emancipation overlaps with feminism, the latter expressing strong and at times aggressive and violent feelings against men. At the extreme end of feminism there is a desire for total independence from men, taking full charge of their own lives, a liberation from male control and an attack on marriage and the family as symbols of women's enslavement. These views do not represent the position of the majority of women who aspire to an equality of worth with equity in opportunities for work, position and a more egalitarian relationship with men. All these aspirations are in keeping with the basic Christian belief that men and women are created in the image of God and are of equal worth, destined for a life of mutual dignity, achieved through the complementarity of the sexes. Thus the very best of the emancipation ideology is in keeping with Christian views about human beings.

The emancipation of women is not mere theory. During the Second World War women participated extensively in the work effort. After the war they entered the labour force in huge numbers, and one of the features of the last twenty-five years has been their large-scale employment. This employment has had many repercussions. The working woman has an economic independence not present in her unemployed sister. It is true that often her income enters the family budget, but in theory at least, it means that she is not obliged to stay in an impossible marital situation for economic reasons. Work however is not merely a source of remuneration. It is an activity that offers companionship, a source of social identity and the growth of self-confidence. Thus through work women gain the double advantage of economic freedom and personal significance which in turn shapes their role in marriage. If they feel that marriage is destroying them, they can come out of it much more easily than before.

Work has not been the only great change in women's lives. Since the early sixties the advent of the contraceptive pill has produced a revolution in family life. Widespread and safe birth regulation, now for the first time largely under control of the wives, means that childbearing has also been brought under greater control than ever before. The timing of pregnancy has meant that women often have their children reasonably early in marriage and are then free to concentrate on work. Furthermore the size of the family has been reduced to an average of two children, so that one of the main reasons for women being at home has been greatly reduced.

The large-scale entry of women into work, coupled with reduction of the size of the family, has meant that their world has become opened to new and broader horizons and their image of themselves has been enhanced. This change has had repercussions within marriage, where wives have naturally expected a similar widening of involvement with their husbands in consultation, discussion and decision making. The power between the sexes has had a redistribution with its axis shifting in the direction of wives. It is not surprising that women expect more from marriage, and their dissatisfaction is often expressed in petitioning for divorce. In fact currently seven out of ten petitions are filed by women who have ultimately found the relationship incompatible with their minimum expectations.

Expectations have risen not only for women, who have been spear-heads in the changing nature of marriage. Other factors have been operating which have involved both men and women. The post-war era has seen a marked rise in living standards which are only now beginning to subside, even though material standards remain high in 30—40 per cent of the world which comprise the countries of the West. In these countries the challenges of adequate provision of food, shelter, employment and social security, education and health have been met to a considerable degree. When basic needs of survival are reached, human beings imperceptibly seek fulfilment at a deeper layer of their being, where the world of feelings, emotions and sexuality are engaged. Both sexes, but once again particularly women, expect more in the way of fulfilment at this level. Christians have been wary of this movement. Christianity has been influenced a great deal by the emphasis on reason which has been such a predominant influence in Western society. The advent of a much stronger emphasis on the affective aspect of life has been received with a mixture of welcome and caution. But even this apprehensive reception has not been matched by educational advances focusing on the training of feelings and emotions. Thus one of the consequences is that both sexes are intuitively moving towards the world of feelings without proper social and psychological preparation.

If Christianity has been apprehensive about feelings, it has been even more anxious about sexuality, a subject to which Christianity has never given the care it deserves. The post-war era has seen a massive extension of interest in sexual matters as the studies of Kinsey, Masters and Johnson and other sexologists invaded society. This reawakening of interest, coupled with the arrival of safe and cheap birth regulation, has produced an explosion of the so-called 'permissive society' in the last twenty-five years. The majority of couples did not indulge in this permissive scene in which spouse-swapping, open marriage, triangular arrangements and orgies captured the headlines. Nevertheless a change took place for the silent majority. Husbands and increasingly wives recognized the importance of sex in marriage and were no longer content to remain in sexually arid situations. The rise in sexual therapy, more prominent in the United States than in Britain, is an indication that marital partners do expect more in this area of their life.

The increased importance given to the intimate and personal aspects of the marital relationship is also associated with the great advances that psychology and psychiatry have made in the post-war world. The ideas of such men as Freud, Jung and Adler have penetrated widely in society. Concepts such as 'inferiority complex', 'sexual drive', 'instincts', 'psychoanalysis', 'defences', 'subconscious' have become part of everyday language. Human relations are viewed increasingly against this background of sophistication from the psychological sciences and, although marriage has not been affected too deeply by these ideas, it has certainly been influenced by them. One of the important aspects of the influence of Freud and his sexual theories has been the popular belief that sexual abstention is damaging. In fact Freud never said anything of the sort and he was careful not to reduce the importance of moral rules and regulations. Nevertheless naive interpretations of his writings have led to simplistic conclusions that life without sex is harmful. No evidence exists for this belief, but its dissemination in certain quarters has meant that pre- and extra-marital sex have come to be viewed with a tolerance that is in direct conflict with Christian views of sexuality.

Whilst all these innovations are altering the expectations and behaviour of married couples, the deterrents against experiment and dissolution have been weakened. The influence of Christian standards has undoubtedly diminished and the constraints that these applied have been greatly reduced. The combination of all this has meant that divorce has soared and the question remains, what the social Christian response should be?

There are those who wish to have nothing to do with these changes and want to return to a fundamental and conservative approach. Such an view is understandable. Christians have always to return to the radical sources of their faith and in this instance they have to preserve life, love and stability in permanent relationships. There are however doubts whether a conservative opposition is the most Christian response. A careful analysis suggests that this is not so in the case of divorce.

An examination of the social reasons, offered in this chapter to understand the changes in marriage, indicates that the last quarter of a century has witnessed a definite shift in the equality of the marital relationship. Against a background of material prosperity, men and women are seeking a more egalitarian and richer experience in marriage. There is a definite rise of what is considered to be the minimum standards that couples can expect from each other. In other words there is a deeper engagement of integrity and love as the affective and psychological component of the personality rises to become integrated with the social. Such a widening of the meaning of love is welcome to Christians who are constantly seeking the fullest possible realization of the image of God in man. There is thus a paradox in the current situation. An approach of deeper commitment to love is associated with a rapid and widespread increase in divorce. The answer is obvious. Christianity cannot turn the clock back nor should it wish to do so. The greater manifestation of love which contemporary marriage is attempting to achieve is occurring against a background of little preparation, education and support for these modern objectives. Christianity is absolutely right in protesting against divorce which, as we have seen in the previous chapter, is an event associated with widespread human suffering. But the response cannot be merely negative. If the analysis presented here is correct, the response must be a clear initiative by the Church to alert society to its responsibilities. If Christianity wants deeper and more fulfilling marriage, then it must give priority to education, training and support for it. In other words the Christian response must be to achieve the fuller aims of contemporary marriage without the severe penalties of divorce. Since the Church remains deeply involved in marriage and the family, it has its own specific contribution to this raising of consciousness about the important striving of contemporary marriage to achieve a deeper level of love. What this contribution should be is considered at the end of this book.

In the meantime however there are a number of questions which the sceptics pose. The case argued so far depends on an interaction between the external social factors and the internal quality of the life of the partners. What happens if material standards drop? What if unemployment persists? Clearly if material standards drop severely and persistently, they are bound to influence the internal life of marriage. Social adversity has a deleterious effect on matrimony but assuming that, even if material standards drop, they will not fall too steeply, then the inner life of marriage will proceed on current lines. Furthermore the aim of Christianity in terms of social justice is to raise the social conditions of the people on the whole face of the earth however long this may take. So that in the long run the authentic social advantages of the West are shared by many others. Even if there are fluctuations in social conditions, the insights gained from psychology and the process of the emancipation of women, both consistent with Christian principles, are not likely to go into reverse. The reasonable conclusion must be that the richer insights gained in the last quarter of a century are likely to remain a permanent part of human understanding and their impact on marriage an enduring consequence to which Christianity must make an adequate response.

This response however must be more than a welcome reception of the changes, for where love is, God is. It must be more than an extended gathering of its resources to understand, educate and support these aspirations. It must also make its unique contribution that any realization of love requires effort, sacrifice and the constant injection of hope which is an intrinsic part of Christian belief. These specific Christian contributions have to counter cynicism and the belief that the contemporary aspirations can be achieved easily, without persistent effort, patience, understanding, education and support.

Specific social factors

The broad social changes described above provide the background against which scientists have examined a number of specific social factors. These are concerned with courtship, age at marriage, pre-marital pregnancy, social class, religion and mixed backgrounds.

1. *Courtship*

If parents are no longer responsible for matching the necessary attributes of young people in order to have a successful marriage, then the couple themselves have to do it in the process called courtship. Social scientists argue how courtship proceeds from the initial meeting to the wedding ceremony. Leaving aside the actual details, it is a process which involves various phases of greater intimacy. Physical and social attraction play an initial part and there is plenty of evidence that couples come together who have similar social characteristics of background, education and class.

This ensures that there is no marked disparity in social factors and allows for easy interaction. If, in this interaction, liking progresses to the feeling that 'I would like to be with this man/woman for life', then love enters the relationship and gradually leads to marriage. Courtship is a process which often lasts between one and two years and during this time there is a constant checking and rechecking of attraction, suitability, complementarity and blending together. It is a vital time, and the quality of courtship is intimately linked with the outcome of the marriage. There are some features which are associated with increased risk to the marriage.

Short courtships are in fact linked with marital instability. Couples who marry after knowing each other for a few days or weeks are taking considerable risks. This does not mean that some do not fall in love at first sight or early in their acquaintance, but this feeling needs to be tested in the course of a fuller experience. Stormy relationships are also poor omens for the future. Frequent arguments indicate that there is a basic difference of approach to something of importance and, unless the conflict is resolved before the marriage, it is likely to continue afterwards. Frequent arguments may be due to such matters as excessive drinking, gambling or jealousy. There are men and women who recognize their partner has a problem, e.g. alcoholism, and yet they proceed with the marriage on the basis that their 'love' will prove strong enough to change the situation after marriage. This is a mistaken approach. The doubt is not about the strength of their love, but the capacity and freedom of their partner to change. It is much better to insist that the habit should change before marriage rather than afterwards.

The same principles apply to sexual behaviour. If the partner leads a promiscuous life during courtship, it is likely that this will continue after marriage and such an outcome should not surprise the future spouse.

There is one more feature about courtship which stands out in the history of broken marriages and is of a vital importance. Many men and women whose marriage fails say clearly that they were never in love with their spouse when they married them. Some of this thinking is a rationalization but a good deal is not. Men and women, particularly the latter, remember clearly that they were unsure about proceeding with the marriage. They were not in love and often it was their spouse who did the running and persisted in their intention. If the doubt against marriage is strong and the hesitation amounted to an actual withdrawal, then in some cases the refused person threatens to commit suicide or even makes a gesture as a way of reversing the decision. If the decision is reversed, then the consequences may be disastrous.

So how does one decide whether to proceed or not with marriage, particularly as many people have last-moment doubts and hesitations? The answer is not clear, but there are indications of how to decide. Many men and women have last-minute anxiety about a wedding and even a sense of panic. But when they examine their feelings closely, their panic is not about the person they intend to marry but rather about getting married. This is an understandable reaction and, as long as there is no fundamental doubt about the partner, the marriage can proceed. But when the doubts are about the person, then caution should prevail. If there are persistent anxieties about the future spouse, then it is better to withdraw even at the last moment. The danger in proceeding with such a marriage is that clearly there is no real freedom of choice and a certain coercion exists. Years later the coerced person will feel free from the emotional pressures of their spouse and will fall in love for the first time in their life. They will then be sorely tempted to break up the marriage and pursue an alternative life with their lover.

Given all these difficulties and the actual number of marriages that end in divorce, a number of young people have decided to live together for a period of time, or even permanently, rather than to marry. Allowing for the difficulty of deciding precisely what constitutes living together, nevertheless the practice has increased in recent years. It is far too early to say whether this practice protects against marital breakdown but those who imagine that living together makes couples immune to difficulties are seriously mistaken. Living together has its own problems and in many marriages which later run into difficulties, the spouses had previously lived together.

2. *Age at marriage*

If brief and stormy courtships are poor indicators of marital stability, then youthful marriages are even more likely to end in divorce. Studies from all over the world have shown that marriages under the age of twenty carry a high risk of future marital dissolution. This is not surprising. Couples in such marriages have reached physical and intellectual maturity but certainly not an equivalent emotional one. Since emotions are playing such an increasing role in marriage, then the relative immaturity is an important adverse factor. Furthermore marriages at this age are associated with housing, work and economic disadvantages. The combination of these with emotional difficulties may load the marriage with insurmountable difficulties.

3. *Pre-marital pregnancy*

Another factor that has been linked with marital instability is pre-marital pregnancy and the coupling of this factor with a youthful marriage provides one of the most serious combinations that can damage a marriage. The reasons for this are not difficult to discern. A pre-marital pregnancy forced many a marriage in the past. Increasingly it is realized that this must not happen. A pregnancy is not a compelling reason to marry unless the couple are in love and wish to do so. Furthermore when a couple marry with a pre-marital or early pregnancy their world is restricted by the needs of the child and a lot of anger may be mobilized against each other. The mother in particular may have to give up her job to look after the baby and bitterly resent this while blaming the father for what happened.

One solution to this predicament is abortion. This is not a Christian answer. Life is sacred and precious, and the task of the church is to protect it and support the single mother if needs be.

4. *Social class*

Much evidence suggests that the lowest socio-economic groups have the highest divorce rate, although studies in Britain have also indicated that Class III non-manual is also vulnerable. The high rate of divorce in the lower socio-economic group may be a reflection of a combination of factors such as the fact that this group marry early, which is a high-risk factor, and is also associated with many social disadvantages.

5. *Religion*

It would be expected that those who have strong religious beliefs and practice their faith are likely to have lower divorce rates and this is the case. Religious affiliation in itself which is not associated with active expression is no protection. Those who are baptized or are nominal believers in their faith are no different in the outcome of their marriage from those who have no faith. It is the commitment and practice of a faith that disapproves of divorce which is protective.

6. *Mixed background*

There was a time when mixed backgrounds of religion, race, ethnic, social class all carried a higher risk of divorce. Today it is much more acceptable to marry outside one's background and the social disadvantages have lessened. Nevertheless a great deal still can be said for similarity of social background. The reason for this is that, in the presence of the inevitable difficulties in marriage, dissimilar social backgrounds enhance the problems. If a couple with different backgrounds wish to marry, extra care should be taken to ensure that they do agree about the fundamentals of their future married life.

These special social factors should be background knowledge in any preparation for marriage. If adverse factors are present, the couple should be appraised of them and helped to understand and appreciate their possible destructive contribution to the future marriage. In some instances the timetable of marriage may be altered by delaying the marriage. Sometimes the marriage may be postponed indefinitely. If the marriage is to continue as anticipated, such a couple should receive special support in the early years of their marriage when the risks will be at their highest.

Further reading

Changes in Marriage and the Family:

J. Dominian, *Marriage, Faith and Love.* Darton, Longman and Todd, 1981.
Change in Marriage. National Marriage Guidance Council, 1982.
R. N. Rapoport, M. P. Fogarty and R. Rapoport (editors) for the British Committee on Family Research, *Families in Britain.* Routledge and Kegan Paul, 1982.
E. Shorter, *The Making of the Modern Family.* Collins, London, 1976.

The Contribution of Specific Social Factors:

B. Thornes and J. Collard, *Who Divorces?* Routledge and Kegan Paul, 1979.

FOUR

The Psychological Factors

Dynamic features

In the previous chapter the general and specific social factors which have contributed to changes in marriage were examined. In this chapter the psychological factors are considered, but before doing so it is necessary to bring the social and psychological changes together and to see what type of marriage takes shape. It has been noted that two features stand out in the social changes. One is the movement associated with the emancipation of women and the second is the emergence of great emphasis on companionship with its implicit assumption that feelings, emotions and sexuality have an increased importance. Research evidence suggests that these two features have combined to produce a new type of marriage which has to be contrasted with the more traditional form.

Traditionally marriage was a religious and legal arrangement whose chief feature was the fulfilment of certain roles by the spouses. Thus the husband was considered to be the head of the family, the person who went out to work, looked after the material needs of his wife and children, was consulted in all major decisions and when necessary negotiated the external commitments of the family. The wife and children were meant to accept his authority and show him suitable respect for his pre-eminent position. The wife's chief task was to bear the children, to take care of them and to be the catalyst of affection, subordinate to her husband. The essence of marriage was the discharge of these duties and, provided the couple fulfilled these roles and remained faithful to each other, they were considered to have a good marriage. Often love did enter such a marriage but it was not a prerequisite.

Gradually this picture of marriage is changing. The

emancipation of women has influenced the man-woman relationship and the pre-eminence of the husband is giving way as the spouses have a more egalitarian relationship. This means several things. It implies that power is shared and decisions are not reached unilaterally but are the result of joint consultation. Consultation in turn means talking, discussing, examining issues from different angles. Here there is potentially a problematic area. Some spouses, particularly men, may have a dominant make-up and find such exchange intolerable. They like to make decisions unfettered by consultation, and this may be unacceptable to their wives. When discussion does take place men like to examine the rational basis of the issue under consideration, and consider the appropriate action. Women do not wish to confine themselves to these aspects alone; they want to evaluate the intuitive, feeling side of the subject. For men their approach appears 'commonsense', but for women 'commonsense' is more than thinking; it is feeling, sensing and intuition. Thus joint decisions have to blend both aspects of the personality. In practice the majority of couples learn from each other and mutually enrich themselves. Trouble surfaces when one, or the other, or both, cannot comprehend their partner's approach. Instead of trying to learn from each other, they tend to dismiss, deprecate and attack the other's point of view. In order to protect their perception of life, they attempt to destroy the version of the other. Such attacks are interpreted as potentially destructive and they are received as 'put downs' or 'rejections' of the basic self.

This egalitarian approach of the spouses also means that their relationship is a more intimate one. They are no longer separated by roles, status and fixed positions which are complementary. Roles are being gradually replaced by inter-action of persons with a much greater degree of closeness to each other. This intimacy has profound psychological implications whose roots stem from the world of psychoanalysis.

Freud was the first person to show clearly that when a therapist sees a patient many times a week then a transference develops. By transference is meant that, in the intimacy of the therapeutic relationship, the patient relives their childhood experiences and treats their therapist as a significant figure from their childhood, usually a parent but anyone else may also be experienced. The patient relives childhood experiences of conflict, anger, love, anxiety, sexual feelings, deprivation, etc. Freud used this reactivation of feelings, both conscious and unconscious, as a second opportunity to analyse their meaning.

This analysis offers many possibilities. Unconscious feelings are rendered conscious and can thus be integrated for the first time with the rest of the personality. Distortions can be corrected. Above all there is a second chance to experience love, care, attention from a therapist who is prepared to make these available. Thus transference can have a profound healing effect. But transference is not confined to the analytical couch, it occurs wherever two people have a continuous and intimate relationship, and contemporary marriage is one such relationship. Spouses experience each other not only as husband and wives but as fathers and mothers and occasionally as other significant persons such as grandparents and other relatives.

Modern marriage par excellence lends itself to be the second intimate relationship in life, the first one being between ourselves and our parents. In this second relationship, as in psychoanalysis and psychotherapy, we relive our original conflicts, anger, need for love, anxieties, fear of rejection, insecurities, sexual feelings, etc. All marriages undergo this transference to a variable degree and the interaction can have a major healing effect, as it plainly does in the majority of marriages. But unresolved emotional problems can overwhelm the couple. So, in marriage counselling, the childhood experiences of the couple are an essential part for understanding the current emotional difficulties.

So far the intimacy of the relationship has been emphasized, but contemporary marriage has to facilitate both this intimacy and the integrity of the husband and wife as persons. Couples do not wish to remain in each other's arms all day long. They come together for consultation, mutual support, decision making, social activity, sexual encounter; at other times they need to feel free to think, act, pursue their own interests and have time to be themselves. Contemporary marriage is a delicate balance between closeness and separateness, not only in terms of activity but in the emotional pressures couples place on each other. As we shall see the commonest complaint in marriage is the absence of closeness in terms of time together, recognition of one's inner world, accurate response to it and good communication. But there are marital difficulties which are concerned with the question of separateness. Wives in particular feel suffocated by husbands who are jealous, possessive and will not allow them to work, who control and dominate their lives and want them solely to meet their needs. When such women have young children as well they feel all their time and emotions are soaked up by the needs of their husband and children, leaving them with nothing for themselves. Possessiveness is not of course entirely a male characteristic. There are wives who also feel jealous, fearful of being abandoned, anxious, who find it impossible to let their husbands out of their sight and are for ever complaining of being ignored.

The ideal, towards which contemporary marriage is moving, is that of an egalitation relationship with companionship predominating and the couple having a balanced interaction, in which closeness and separateness meet their needs for oneness and individuality. This calls for a tremendous amount of understanding, flexibility, compromise, mutual facilitation and a continuous awareness of the changes in each other which demand adjustment. It has been found that rigid, uncompromising, unyielding, immature, sensitive personalities are not suited to these flexible demands of marriage, and we need to examine how this interaction is influenced by some features of the personality.

Personality factors

1. *Dependence-dominance*
Attempting to define the personality has been a feature present in all cultures since the beginning of historical records. The human personality is so rich and varied that to capture its essentials in full is an impossible task. Nevertheless it is possible to describe an outline which is relevant to the marital relationship.

Observing the growth of the personality, the first feature that stands out is the dependence of the child on the parents. The child experiences mother and father as the source of provision of food, security and love, which for most of childhood appears to be going in one direction from parent to child. In marriage this dependence continues, and there are men and women who marry primarily to receive attention, care and love for which they have an excessive need. If they marry someone who is equally deprived, they rapidly exhaust that person's limited resources. If they marry a nurturing husband or wife, the relationship can thrive but it has its problems. If the wife is the nurturing person, then her husband can have her exclusive attention until the children come, at which point the demands on her rise. Now her resources have to be shared and, if the husband finds the reduction difficult, problems start. He begins to feel that his wife has changed and is no longer fully available, something which he finds difficult to understand or to accept. He becomes sullen and angry and she feels exhausted and resentful. Irritability rises, quarrels multiply and anger permeates the atmosphere, something that happens wherever there is marital conflict. The husband has to be helped to see the change in circumstances and learn for the time being to reduce his needs. The arrival of children is the commonest and most obvious reduction in availability on the part of the wife, but the same thing may happen when she is ill, depressed, preoccupied with other events or tired, and the same tensions may arise. Equally the husband may be the nurturing spouse and his attention may be diluted by similar factors causing the wife to feel neglected.

As we grow, our emotional dependence becomes less, in the sense that we can cope with periods of less intense reception of attention and this is an aspect of the maturing person. This maturity is also developed in other psychological and social aspects. Other psychological features of this maturity are our abilities to delay gratification compared with the earlier need for immediate satisfaction, to cope with frustration without panicking or getting into a rage and to handle criticism without feeling rejected. We learn to cope with disappointment and to persevere against adversity without feeling overwhelmed or reverting to an earlier state of dependence, seeking help from the 'strong partner'. In terms of social competence, we learn how to mix in company, retain friends, cope with money, accept responsibility for our actions, evaluate competing demands, allocate priorities and ultimately handle work. The immature person cannot do these things, and the husband who is immature finds it difficult to stay at work and to handle money; he gets into debt, is afraid to accept responsibility for household tasks or repairs, is constantly asking what to do and treats his wife as a mother who is there to run his life and protect him. In these circumstances the wife has to handle the money, pay the bills, look after the maintenance of the house, and even at times take care of the family financially. If the wife is immature, she finds it difficult to look after the house, to do her shopping, supervise the children and gives up in anxiety or depression. She turns to her mother and husband for help and finds it very difficult to keep going.

So far the emotional and social aspects of growth have been considered. There is also a third element, namely that of power. Children feel helpless and easily frightened. Parents have power, authority, competence, are tall and strong in comparison to the physical, social and psychological structure of the child. This strength-weakness dimension has many descriptions in psychology, the commonest being called dominant-dependent, or dominant-passive relationships. Married couples show many features of dominance-dependence. Generally this is a complementary pattern which is most beneficial. In practice it means that each partner has strengths which meet the deficiences of the other and there is mutual enrichment. Difficulties begin when the person who is dominant wants to control and dictate the life of their spouse or in those situations in which the dependent partner refuses or cannot mature and assume normal responsibilities for their life.

2. *Extrovert-introvert*

The dimension of extroversion and introversion is a popular and widely held view of the personality. It is mentioned here because it has some affinities with the dominant-non-dominant dimension. The extrovert person is sociable, mixes easily, has the ability to talk, takes charge of social situations, is interested in people, appears to lack shyness, takes the initiative, is often infused with enthusiasm and gaiety and has charm. The introvert on the other hand, is socially withdrawn, quiet, does not easily get involved with others, can be a loner and is preoccupied with his/her inner world. Jung and Eysenk are two psychologists who have expounded these traits. There is no doubt that opposites can attract and the extrovert-introvert interaction can often be seen in marriage. Extroverts give the impression of being confident, secure, in charge of themselves, and they attract shy, introvert spouses who are seeking extrovert qualities but also are marrying on the implicit assumption that their partner will be 'strong', 'mature', 'decisive'. In fact, as Eysenk indicates, extroverts can be very anxious people and also very insecure. Thus the introvert spouse who marries the extrovert on the basis of their outward manifestations of confidence may find the extrovert's inner world does not match their external appearance. The tables are then reversed with the introvert partner having to support their so-called 'strong' spouse. The discovery of the limitations of the extrovert personality can be a shock which amounts to a betrayal and is one of the reasons for early dissolution of marriage.

3. *Anxiety*

Anxiety is a normal reaction to threatening situations and has a protective element. Everyone has a certain degree of anxiety which increases in frightening and life-endangering situations. A proportion of the population, which may be as high as 30 per cent, has an excessive tendency to be anxious, and this may be due to genetic or environmental factors. The anxious person worries about trivialities and takes a long time to lose their excessive anxiety, the result being that they are continuously under stress. Such a person needs a partner who can accept their anxiety, is supportive and reassuring, and, by being reliable, predictable and trustworthy, is careful not to trigger off more anxiety. The combination of an anxious spouse and a partner who returns from work at all hours of the night, says one thing and does or means another, breaks their promises, is unfaithful, betrays trust, is a recurrent marital problem situation. The anxious spouse needs security and trust to survive, and, if their partner's behaviour arouses more anxiety and mistrust, such a relationship is not viable in the long run.

Anxiety manifests itself in many forms. In technical terms, another feature of anxiety can be its obsessionality.

Obsessional people are perfectionists in the pejorative sense of that word. The need for perfection does not arise from a desire to accomplish to the highest standards but from the anxiety generated by imperfection. Anything imperfect, incomplete or disorderly causes anxiety, and such a person behaves in an excessively tidy, meticulous, perfectionist way. It is the rigidity of these people that produces difficulties. This is the personality that makes wives so obsessed with order and cleanliness that their home assumes the character of an operating theatre where sterility and order are demanded. Children cannot play or make a mess, are told off if they come in with dirty shoes or boots, and husbands must be tidy and live in a hygienic atmosphere. Such women have a fetish for bodily cleanliness and will complain about the hygiene of their husband. Sometimes these wives are so disgusted by anything which has the appearance of dirt that sex and semen are found at the very least disagreeable and at worst disgusting. Husbands who are obsessional demand the same degree of order, have meticulous desks or work-shops and become enraged if these are disturbed or interfered with. Spouses who are obsessional can be ridiculously preoccupied with punctuality, always arriving far too early to catch a train, or at a party. If such an obsessional spouse is married to an untidy, unpunctual partner, then there is constant tension and the husband who complains that he is always waiting for his perpetually late wife is a classic example. In its more benign form the obsessional person is for ever worrying that they have left the gas or electricity on, the house unlocked, food in the oven, or something vital in an incomplete and dangerous state. Such a spouse needs clearly a very understanding partner to cope with their anxieties.

Another form anxiety takes is that of excessive fear or phobia. Everybody is familiar with claustrophobia (excessive fear of being shut in) or agoraphobia (an excessive fear of open space). Fears can also be expressed in social situations, and in some marriages the phobic partner avoids social situations and gradually becomes a recluse, insisting that their partner also behaves in this way.

The anxious person may in fact get so frightened, that they will behave as a terrified child. In the midst of their panic, they can cry, shout, scream, throw themselves about and behave in what is technically called a histrionic manner. This behaviour is called by the partner, often the husband, 'hysterical', and the wife is told that she is 'crazy', 'mental' and needs to be locked up. This is a situation which can frequently arise in marriages saturated with tension, fear, anger and hurt. Wives are made to feel that they are mentally ill, when they know that they are in the grip of sheer terror due to their husband's behaviour. Husbands find histrionic behaviour an excuse to believe that the problem is entirely that of their wife and they need not look at themselves and their contribution to the problem. Counsellors, doctors or priests have all to be on their guard not to ally themselves with the 'innocence' of the husband in these circumstances but need to appreciate that the wives are really being pushed beyond their resources. Sometimes it is the husband who cannot cope with his anxiety and behaves histrionically. When pushed to this point either partner can threaten to take their lives, and attempted suicide gestures are not uncommon.

Finally the anxious person is one who feels readily threatened. When their anxiety is activated the world around them is felt to be populated by men and women who are out to hurt, damage or destroy them. This is called a paranoid reaction, and the paranoid personality feels most of the time that they are surrounded by people who want to harm them. They feel slighted with the minimum reason and are constantly ready to protect themselves from the real and imaginary attacks they feel they receive. Such a personality is obviously not one that can easily be accommodated in a marital relationship, particularly if their partner is the object of their suspicions.

Defences

Part of the great contribution of Freud and his daughter, Anna Freud, was the concept of defences. They saw that the instincts of aggression and sexuality mobilized anxiety and the psyche had to cope with this anxiety, just as the body has to cope with infection by mobilizing its defences.

These psychological defences are the means by which the psyche protects itself from being overwhelmed by anxiety arising from any source. *Denial* is a common one. We simply do not acknowledge that something painful or threatening which is causing us anxiety has happened. The very young child who breaks a plate and is surrounded by its pieces denies responsibility for it. The person who has lost a parent or dear friend does not admit to their death. Whenever anxiety rises we simply deny that it is present or is connected with us. There is an inability to cope with the anxiety of responsibility or guilt. Spouses use denial extensively. If they are anxious or afraid of the consequences of their actions or omissions, they simply deny that something has happened or that they are responsible for it. Sometimes the denial is a deliberate lie but often it is a genuine way of coping with stress. The real challenge for the spouse is to distinguish between lying and a genuine denial. There is little point in accusing a spouse of lying when their anxiety is so high that they can only cope by denying their implication. In these circumstances the spouse has to stop attacking and instead attempt to make the atmosphere sufficiently safe for their spouse's anxiety to diminish to the point where they can remember and admit their part in a situation which is threatening. Counsellors are often faced with spouses who are accusing each other of lying, cheating, being irresponsible in the face of a bland denial. It is the counsellor's task to go beyond the moral judgement, the accusation, and bring about an atmosphere where the need for the denial defence is no longer necessary. This opens the way for an honest discussion of the problem which was previously locked in a conflict of accusation and denial.

Another form of denial is the defence of *rationalization.* Instead of facing the anxiety and pain of certain consequences of our or other peoples' behaviour, we make it look safe by offering our 'rational' explanation. Children who don't want to go to school feel ill. Adults who don't want to do something feel ill, or the job is not worth doing or they change their mind. When we are listening to our spouse asking us to do something, telling us an unpleasant aspect about ourselves, complaining about our attitude to the children or the behaviour of relatives or friends, instead of facing the issue we find reasons why we cannot do what is asked of us, or we reconstruct unpleasant facts facing us and do not accept the implications that are staring in our face. An essential part of rationalization, as the word implies, is the reconstruction of the event or experience in a rational way to remove its threatening quality. This of course can play havoc within a marital relationship when one or both spouses insist on seeing the same thing in a completely different way from that presented by their partner.

The need for reducing anxiety is taken further with the process of *projection*. In this defence we tend to push on to others experiences and particularly feelings which belong to us. Thus it is not we who are angry but our partner. It is not we who are afraid but our partner. It is not we who are telling lies but our partner, and so on. Of course both partners can project on to each other those aspects of themselves which they cannot face. As a result, sometimes spouses find themselves the recipients of all the 'bad' feelings of their partner and have gradually to disentangle their real identity from the one which has been foisted on to them. Spouses may gradually realize that they are not lazy, unloving, indifferent, incompetent, but that these and the many other negative qualities of which they are accused really belong to their partner, who cannot accept their presence. Once again spouses can confuse each other with their mutual projections to the point where they do not know who they are. Counsellors have to untangle these projections and help the couples face honestly their limitations which they project on to their partner.

Another defence is called *reaction formation*. In this defence we reach the conclusion that we do not like something which we cannot cope with. If a behaviour, feeling or phantasy is too stressful, we simply change it by converting it into its opposite characteristic. If we cannot cope with sexual activity, we declare sex to be dirty, wrong or wicked. If we have a problem with rebelling, we can take a vow of obedience or make ourselves excessively submissive and co-operative. In marriage a husband or wife may be accustomed to their partner's reaction formation and gradually have to adjust to the change as the reaction formation gives way to the true feelings of the person. Women and men who are excessively co-operative, willing and yielding at the beginning of their marriage may gradually assert themselves to the surprise of their spouses. Reaction formation fades imperceptibly into sublimation when a person actually and successfully converts an impulse, sexual or aggressive, into another form of creative activity. In marriage the man or woman who is not interested in sex and uses all their energy to be successful at work or in creative art may offer such an example.

All these defences aim to remove the anxiety created by impulses or other aspects of behaviour. The most fundamental way of doing this is to remove the unpleasant feeling of anxiety consciously from awareness by the process of suppression which is a conscious process and by the mechanism of repression which is unconscious. Defences can be effective but are often precarious, and when this is the case the best thing for a couple is to talk openly about their problems and reduce their level of anxiety. At the extreme end of repression, the stress becomes so marked that it can express itself in a psychological form, such as loss of memory or in a physical form, such as the loss of function of a voice, a limb or any other part of the body. These are extremely rare reactions and are usually the concern of psychiatrists.

Counselling

It can be seen that psychological factors are absolutely crucial in marital interaction. At the surface level couples have to relate with their normal personality, and if this is grossly defective then the marriage is likely to run into serious difficulties. Within the confines of the normal personality interaction, a couple have to appreciate each other's defences and create an atmosphere of safety which allows the facing of anxiety without having recourse to defences which really alienate. Finally within the confines of the personality and its defences, the couple have to handle their dynamic needs arising from their childhood.

No marriage counselling can take place without an awareness of these three levels of psychological interaction which are summed up in the personality, defences and dynamic needs. The personality allows the moment-to-moment interaction. When this interaction creates too much anxiety, defences are brought into operation. Often the reason why anxiety rises is due to the fact that important needs of the couple are not being met, and some of these needs stem from childhood. The task of marriage counselling is to help the couple recognize that their relationship is in distress because, instead of their basic needs being met, each spouse is defending their own position and attacking that of the other. Counselling aims to substitute the attacks by mutual understanding of what the real needs are and why they are not being met. As a result of effective counselling there is a shift from anger to good will, from accusations to understanding of the real situation. Finally there comes a proper evaluation of what needs are appropriate and can be met and which are inappropriate and cannot be met.

Further reading

J. A. C. Brown, *Freud and the Post-Freudians.* Penguin, 1969.

E. H. Erikson, *Childhood and Society.* Penguin, 1965.

A. Freud, *The Ego and the Mechanisms of Defence.* Hogarth Press, 1966.

J. H. Kahn, *Human Growth and Development of Personality.* Pergamon Press, 1971.

R. D. Laing, *The Divided Self.* Pelican, 1970.

H. W. Maier, *Three Theories of Child Development.* Harper and Row, 1969.

E. Rayner, *Human Development.* Allen and Unwin, 1978.

C. R. Rogers, *On Becoming a Person.* Constable, 1961.

D. W. Winnicott, *The Family and Individual Development.* Tavistock Publications, 1968.

FIVE

Contemporary Marriage

The heart of marital conflict is the inability to initiate a relationship or to maintain it when essential needs are not being met. One of the reasons for increasing marital breakdown is because these needs or expectations are changing, in fact increasing, and the resources of individuals and society to meet them have not extended with equal rapidity. If the gap is to be bridged, then the inner world of contemporary marriage needs to be clarified and defined as accurately as possible. The attempt to understand the inner world of marriage has been one of my principal concerns, and in this chapter I describe my main conclusions in an abbreviated form.

Sustaining

The essential feature of marriage is the presence of a relationship between a man and woman. This relationship is first and foremost a sustaining experience. This sustaining is social, emotional, sexual, intellectual and spiritual.

At the social level a couple provide company for each other, do things together, meet their relations and friends, entertain and participate in the wider community of the neighbourhood. Some of these activities are carried out separately but they remain available to each other for support. As a married couple they set up a home, run it on the basis of complementary responsibility and most important of all sustain each other economically. This task used to be principally that of the husband and in many ways still remains so, but the wife also contributes nowadays. For the majority of women, work ceases when they have young children and the economic sustaining then falls entirely on the husband. Traditionally, economic support was considered one of the crucial tasks of marriage allocated to the husband.

Currently, however, there is a desire to move beyond economic sustaining and the undertaking of the traditional roles of husband and wife. Emotional sustaining is emerging to be just as important. In the intimate world of contemporary marriage, couples want increasingly to be understood in the depths of their being. They want their partner to feel and appreciate how they experience life and to respond accurately to their mood, feelings and emotions. Ideally, men and women, but particularly the latter, want their partner to be in tune with their inner world, sometimes without saying anything, just as they felt their mother or father understood them in their early years. Often spouses are very good at doing this, but sometimes they find this intuitive insight very difficult, and in this case problems arise. When couples are in tune with each other they know instinctively when to talk and when to keep silent, when the other's mood is low and they need comfort, when they are angry and need pacification, when confused and require clarification of their inner world and so on. This emotional sustaining is gradually acquiring the same significance as the material sustaining used to hold in the past. Not that the need for economic support has disappeared — the two now overlap.

Intellectually and spiritually couples can survive with totally independent views of life but they prefer to have their points of view appreciated and if possible shared.

The sexual sustaining is a complex phenomenon which will be examined later. It forms the background against which the rest of the sustaining takes place.

Healing

In the presence of this intimate sustaining, the inner world of the couple is gradually exposed to each other. One of the crucial revelations is the presence of hurt, pain and distress. Couples bring to each other some twenty years of accumulated wounds, as well as having to deal with new ones which arise in the course of their marriage.

The basic wounds are those which developed in childhood and they are of three sorts. Physical wounds consist of familiar defects in hearing, seeing and inherited illnesses. Intellectually there may be limited intelligence or specific cognitive defects. But it is emotionally that the most important wounds exist. These may be genetically determined, influencing mood, the tendency to get depressed, elated or anxious; the personality, the tendency to be cold, unemotional, withdrawn, to be controlled, relaxed or aggressive. Wounds may also be acquired in the course of development, through the influence of parents or other key figures in the life of the child.

These wounds are particularly relevant in marriage because they influence the capacity to relate. Thus a spouse may grow up with a domineering mother or father rendering them incapable of taking the initiative, making decisions or feeling competent. They may grow up in a rejecting atmosphere feeling unwanted, unappreciated and unloved or be jealous of a brother or sister who receives greater attention. Even worse a child may grow feeling unworthy, bad and excessively guilty, considering themselves incapable of loving others or worthy of the love of others. These wounds may combine with anxiety, shyness, lack of confidence and produce men and women who feel unlovable, unwanted, easily rejected, who find it difficult to express affection or receive it. Although the extreme forms of these problems affect only a small number of individuals, many people have some of these features, so that there are few marriages in which aspects of these difficulties do not emerge.

In the depths of the revealed intimacy of the contemporary marriage, these wounds become part of the shared world of the couple. What the wounded person desires is healing and the person they expect it from is their spouse. Men and women who feel insignificant want recognition. The unappreciated and rejected desire to feel wanted, needed and appreciated. The anxious want reassurance. The shy and withdrawn long for encouragement. The hesitant and those lacking confidence seek confirmation of their talents. Usually a couple's wounds are dissimilar and they can offer to each other the missing components of their personality. The confident husband reassures his wife about her significance. The loving wife gives her husband the experience of being wanted and appreciated. The shy husband or wife is encouraged by their partner. In a whole variety of ways complementarity goes on and healing is achieved. We are just beginning to appreciate that marriage is a most powerful, if not the commonest, and most significant source of healing in the community.

The implications for the Christian faith are monumental. Marriage has always been seen as something holy, a relationship initiated and confirmed by God and, in the Roman Catholic tradition, it is recognized as a sacrament. One of the central beliefs of Christianity is that God heals, through his Son and the Holy Spirit, and in fact the Holy Trinity is present and operates in marriage. This presence of grace is not a mysterious, indefinable entity. It has definite expression in the changes it brings about in the participants of marriage, and one way it operates is through the healing outlined. Those who do not believe in Christianity are not excluded from the grace of God and for them the 'miracle' of transformation is interpreted as the result of love.

Healing takes place when the needs of one partner can be met, at least partially, by the resources of the other. When both partners have similar wounds and few resources, then healing is difficult and in these circumstances the counsellor may have to provide some of the resources by injecting feelings of hope and encouragement in the relationship. Ultimately however the desire for healing becomes an expectation. It is seen as a part of the relationship which should be met, and if it is totally neglected it forms the grounds for some divorces.

Growth

One feature of contemporary marriage is the fact that it lasts much longer than in the past. Current marriages continue some fifty years and those who criticize permanency and faithfulness maintain that this is an exceedingly long time for couples to stay together and remain faithful to each other. This would be true if matrimony was visualized as a static, legal arrangement in which the partners are trapped in an unchanging relationship with each other for half a century. This is how traditional marriages could be interpreted, if they are seen as contracts entered into merely for the fulfilment of roles, but this is not the case. Marriages are relationships which express the growing and changing aspirations of the couple. Growth and change are inescapable aspects of marriage. Most partners facilitate this transformation by sharing their life and both encouraging and accepting each new phase. Growth is built on the acceptance by one's self and one's partner of the *status quo* and the mutual recognition and enhancement of further development which generates further potential. Continuity of a relationship allows this process to take place in an uninterrupted way. Husbands and wives come to know each other very well, accept what is good and encourage changes which promote the personality in its further development. When marriages break down, this intimate mutual knowledge is lost and each has to start afresh building a common knowledge of their resources and deficits with a new partner. Sometimes the first spouse is so critical, insensitive and unhelpful that a second relationship is a necessity if growth is to occur. But ideally one relationship allows continuous and uninterrupted development based on the best available mutual insights of further potential growth. One of the features of marriage counselling is to recognize when growth is blocked in one or both partners and to unblock and free the process afresh without the breakdown of the marriage. This necessitates helping one partner to recognize that the other is changing and needs new responses from them. Often the growth of a partner is resisted because there is the fear that it will lead to their ultimate departure or it will make life so different that the relationship will alter radically. Examples of this will be given in chapter 10.

In what ways do couples grow? They can change physically, intellectually, socially, emotionally and spiritually.

Physical growth in terms of absolute size ceases towards the end of the second decade, but the skills of the body can go on developing for a lifetime in athletic and game proficiency, in creative and artistic talents — be they carpentry, cooking, sewing, gardening—and in many other spheres. For this growth to take place the spouse needs encouragement, the sacrifice of togetherness to allow further training and appreciation of the fruits of their achievement.

Intellectually, young people reach the limits of their intelligence at the same time as they complete their physical growth, but intelligence needs to be gradually transformed into wisdom, and this takes a life time. Intelligence provides the means for reflecting and evaluating one's own ideas and those of others. These ideas are constantly influenced by what we read, hear and see, and wisdom is the culmination of the process whereby the truth is appreciated in its greatest possible richness. In troubled marriages we see the inter-action of couples who deny, attack and criticize each other's ideas, leading to a gradual undermining of confidence. But in the majority of marriages the ideas of each other are received with care and concern, and a constant attempt is made to appreciate their worth. In the process of inter-action the good is refined and the defective is gradually eliminated. Once again this growth occurs at its best when ideas are developed continuously in an atmosphere of positive and deepening insight of their meaning.

At the social level growth can take place in a direction in which one partner who finds socializing difficult is gradually encouraged and assisted by the other to mix with people without fear. But in a wider setting both husband and wife can assist each other to take a much greater interest in the life of the community and to undertake service for others. Sometimes this may involve marked sacrifice, when for example the husband gives up a professional or business career to become a priest or to undertake some form of social work.

Emotionally, it involves helping each other to grow in the capacity to love. Loving in marriage includes better communication, greater sensitivity and awareness of each other's world, less criticism and more appreciation, the ability to remain silent at the appropriate moments and not to damage the situation further by impulsive comments, the readiness to accept responsibility and to apologize, coupled with the ability to forgive. Beyond forgiveness love extends to the desire and capacity to help the spouse understand their behaviour and change it to their advantage. Others would find an entirely different set of tenets with which to define love. The important thing is that love can go on growing until the last moment of our lives and has no limitations, being coterminous with the mystery of God's life.

Spiritually, growth takes place as the couple realize that the miracle of their life and love needs explanation. For some people this explanation does not go beyond an appreciation of what is experienced and muted thanksgiving directed to an unknown source. In many others the same miracle is constantly leading them to a sense of the 'beyond', the transcendental where God exists. This God may not be recognized in the traditional way of Christianity but this awareness shapes the faith and values of the partners.

Between them sustaining, healing and growth are gradually forming the internal structure of marriage. Few couples will actually come to a marriage counsellor complaining of the absence of sustaining, healing and growth and using these words, but in fact if their difficulties are listened to with these dimensions in mind, most of their problems fall into expectations which are contained in these three categories. These dimensions also show the immense potential of contemporary marriage and the challenge faced by society to help couples achieve these aims at least in a minimal way. When these aspirations are met, even in minimal terms, the present spate of marital breakdown will abate because the emergent hopes will have been met. An important contribution to the fulfilment of these needs is their introduction at the time of the preparation for marriage so that couples have some idea of what to expect.

The sexual dimension

It has already been mentioned that a greater awareness of sexuality and the realization of its potential is an essential part of the current evolution. The contributors to this change are the sexologists and psychologists who have emphasized the significance of sexuality and the advent of widespread and effective contraception.

The arrival of widely used contraception has implications which go well beyond the ability to control conception. For thousands of years sexuality has been linked with procreation. Now the overwhelming majority of sexual acts are consciously and deliberately not linked with new life. Some have been frightened that this will release an erotic, pleasure-seeking extravaganza. It is true that some freeing of sexuality has taken place, but rampant permissiveness has not occurred and sexual intercourse is still primarily confined within marriage or in loving and exclusive relationships, mostly the former. The question that arises is the meaning of sexuality when it is no longer essentially linked with procreation. What is its purpose then?

Sexual intercourse is essentially a body language. It involves the union of bodies through which a sense of oneness is achieved. The relaxed ease, comprehensive interaction of body and mind are what couples seek. They want to feel relaxed to touch each other, to receive from touch trust and security as they felt when hugged by parents, and at the same time to experience erotic pleasure which gradually becomes a consummated genital union reaching a climax of exquisite pleasure and relief of tension. This forms the background, the bodily connection, through which the couple are talking to each other. Those who are afraid that sex will become simply a sensation of pleasure fail to see that couples who are in love use this pleasure to reach and address each other as persons. What are they saying to each other? What is the text of the sexual language?

First of all successful sexual intercourse elicits a deep sense of gratitude. The couple appreciate what they have received and, with or without words, they say 'thank you' to each other. This thanksgiving may be expressed with a mere grunt or can expand into a rich epilogue but often it is contained in a saturated silence. Thus at the very heart of sexual intercourse there is felt and expressed gratitude.

This gratitude is linked with the desire for repetition. The couple want to repeat the joy the same night, the following day, but in any case, soon. Implicit in this desire is the hope that their partner shares this feeling and wishes to respond in a similar manner. This hope is not merely a matter of wishing to have more pleasure but includes the awareness that through this pleasure they are giving the whole of themselves. Giving however is only one half of the exchange, the other half is receiving. Some sexual difficulties are focused precisely on this ability to give and to receive. Men and women who find it difficult to give of themselves because of the fear of being rebuffed, rejected, overwhelmed, taken over, hold themselves back. Others find it so difficult to believe that anyone wants them, that they cannot accept what is offered to them. But for the overwhelming majority who can mutually donate themselves and receive in return, the union is a rich accomplishment of mutual enhancement.

This mutual enhancement has specific healing qualities. It can extinguish hurt and pain. No couple can escape misunderstanding, conflict, quarrelling and hurt. These quarrels lead rapidly to apology and forgiveness but often a certain amount of hurt remains and sexual intercourse has the capacity of removing it. Thus another feature of love-making is its ability to bring about reconciliation.

All these various existential meanings are possible because the couple are attracted to each other on a sexual basis. Sexual intercourse is the most powerful and economic means through which the spouses' sexuality is reinforced. The man who makes effective love to his wife not only gives her pleasure but through the pleasure confirms that he enjoys her body and her femininity, in other words he confirms repeatedly her sexual identity. In a similar manner she does the same thing for him.

But sexual identity is not the whole person. Through the erotic encounter the husband is saying to his wife that he recognizes, wants and appreciates her as a person and similarly she reciprocates in her feelings. Thus coitus is a most powerful source of recurrent affirmation of each other not only as a sexual being but as a person. Both spouses need this and when it is absent there is a sense of marked frustration. Women in particular complain that husbands, when they fail to surround genital penetration with adequate preparation for love-making, are treating them as sexual objects and not as persons. Both sexes need to feel that they are persons first, before they become sexual beings, and if this does not occur they feel reduced in their meaning.

Thus in the depths of sexual intercourse are to be found the characteristics of thanksgiving, hope, reconciliation, sexual and personal affirmation. Love-making encompasses all these possibilities.

Given this richness of the sexual act, it can easily be seen that it is a powerful reinforcer of the sustaining, healing and growth processes. In addition however it has its own unique meaning. Every time successful intercourse takes place it gives life to the couple. Life and love are linked and are both contained in this activity. Birth regulation has thus helped us to see the rich potential of this act which is laden with meaning, and the union it brings about is a prototype of all forms of unions from the simplest to the divine.

Sexual intercourse has the capacity to give life on each and every occasion, and we are just beginning to realize that this is its most profound purpose. Such a realization is still limited but it is part of the authentic deepening of our understanding of its meaning. Given this richness—which can only be fully realized in a continuous, personal, exclusive relationship—the traditional condemnations against fornication and adultery remain meaningful in a new context. The primary reason for these condemnations is no longer the risk of procreation outside the framework of two supportive parents, nor is it connected with enjoying pleasure without responsibility. The grounds of condemnation are simply that sexual intercourse has such a rich potential to activate human love that only a continuous and exclusive relationship such as marriage can do full justice to it. It is not marriage that makes coitus morally right when it was previously wrong. Coitus belongs to marriage, for it is only in that relationship that its full purpose can be realized.

But what about procreation? There is no doubt at all that children remain important and precious, important if the world is to continue, precious because they are a profound expression of the love of the parents and they elicit further love in their upbringing. The rise of sexual significance does not mean the demise of the procreative aspect of intercourse. It does mean however that everything we know about the education of children indicates that they need stable and loving parents. Sexual intercourse contributes substantially to marital happiness hence its increasing appreciation.

In brief, therefore, sexual intercourse is a life-giving experience. Ninety-nine per cent of the time its life-giving properties are to be found in the interaction of the couple and on a few occasions in the creation of new life. These possibilities of sexual intercourse justify the increasing preoccupation of Western societies with raising the level of sexual practice, because ultimately it is a major contribution to love.

Love

The personal and sexual world of contemporary marriage has been shaped by a variety of social and psychological factors which collectively have raised the level of awareness of the meaning of love in marriage. This has been accompanied by an unprecedented increase in marital breakdown, and the combination of these features forms the paradox of the contemporary marriage situation. The growth in loving potential is, in Christian terms, a better definition and further deepening of the image of God in man and as such is to be welcomed and supported. Divorce is the negative side and it should be resisted, but the resistance should be pursued by educating and supporting couples in their search for this fuller realization of God in man. For those who do not believe in God but wish to experience this deeper love, the same principles of support and education should apply, for ultimately love is the bridge between the two.

The prevention of marital breakdown, which is the *raison d'être* of this book, needs a deep appreciation of the changes in contemporary marriage and the encouragement of the couple's aims as a way of helping men and women to realize their newly desired dimensions of love without having to resort to divorce.

Whatever support the Church and society can give to marriage, its deeper layers cannot be achieved without knowledge of what is involved on the one hand and sustained effort and sacrifice on the other. The common-sense opinion of married couples who have successfully negotiated a lifetime of permanency is that the achievement requires unselfishness, generosity, compromise, persistence and the desire to succeed. These human qualities are present in the overwhelming majority of marriages but, to achieve their objective, they need to be applied to the changing circumstances of the marital relationship. Thus the task of everyone connected with marriage is to be both informed and to guard against easy solutions and shortcuts.

The ideal of contemporary marriage is indeed lofty. Its consummation needs an equivalent degree of insight and perseverance.

Further reading

J. Dominian, *Marriage, Faith and Love.* Darton, Longman and Todd, 1981 (chs. 4, 5, 6, 7 and 8).

PART TWO

SIX

An Approach to Counselling

Introduction

Counselling is a process of helping people which is ultimately derived from psychoanalysis, and many of its features can be traced to the therapeutic technique which Freud initiated. The essentials of that therapy are that the patient lies on a couch with the therapist sitting behind. The patient is allowed complete freedom to express feelings, while the therapist is completely silent and ready to receive what the patient has to say. The feelings that emerge are mostly conscious and deal with everyday life events, but slowly they focus on the way the patient experiences him or herself, others and the therapist. Gradually a greater variety and depth of feelings emerge, particularly about the way the therapist is perceived. This process is assisted by the recalling of dreams, which reveal unconscious material lying outside the immediate awareness of the patient. This material contains feelings and emotions, is intimately linked with love, sex, hate, envy, jealousy, unfulfilled hopes, strivings, feelings of rejection, shame, guilt and distress. Personal injury, the unfulfilled, the damaged and trauma of the past are gradually reached and experienced through the therapist, who is perceived as a key figure, often a parental one. These feelings are often confused, and the task of the therapist is to interpret their meaning and significance, help to remove the emotional defences which have kept them unconscious and allow an integration of the past, present and future to take place.

Thus psychoanalysis is a process in which people are allowed to examine their feelings, both conscious and unconscious, without judgement or advice, in a way that gives them much greater insight and access to themselves. It helps them to integrate feelings and instincts, the conscious and unconscious, the past, present and future, and sets them on a course which frees their energies to realize more fully their potential. Psychoanalysis requires three to five sessions a week lasting several years.

The first modification was that of psychotherapy. The same principles of silent, non-judgemental, non-advisory approach are pursued, and the techniques of listening and interpreting are used. What is listened to and interpreted matters a great deal. Freud emphasized the importance of the instinctual life. Since his day there have been many developments beyond instinctive psychology. The importance of affection, love, hate, security, dependence have been added to anger and sexuality, and these emotions play a crucial part in marital therapy. Psychotherapy usually involves seeing a person once a week, and it tends to focus on conscious objectives. An important development of psychotherapy has been group psychotherapy where half a dozen people come together and use similar techniques.

Between the individual approach of psychoanalysis and psychotherapy and that of group therapy stands the therapy of couples, which is the principal means of helping married people. A further development of couple therapy is that of including the children and other members of the family in what has come to be known as family therapy.

Counselling is a further derivative from these modifications. The individual or the couple are seen face-to-face by the counsellor. The approach is still primarily one of listening to feelings, focusing on those which the couple express about each other in terms of negative and positive reactions, needs and aspirations. In other words a couple are encouraged to communicate what they feel about each other, what is satisfactory and what is not, their mutual needs and how they see their married life. The counsellor is there to facilitate this exchange and help the couple to understand each other. This understanding is crucial, because so often husbands and wives interpret the behaviour of each other in critical, moralistic terms, maintaining that the other behaves in a certain way because they are lazy, selfish, opinionated, uncaring or oppressive. Sometimes spouses are all of these things, but a deeper examination of their behaviour reveals that they are the prisoners of their past. In childhood they learned to behave and react in a certain way, which they bring into their marriage, or their personality makes it difficult for them to relate in the way their spouse wants them to. The counsellor has the task of identifying these factors and helping the partners to appreciate that what is defective stems from genuine limitations and not bad will. Having recognized the gap between need and availability without moral overtones, the task of the counsellor is to facilitate bridging the gap. The principles however are the same. The bridging is not to be achieved primarily by advice — although more will be said about this later — but by assisting the couple to recognize what is missing and to help them motivate themselves to change their behaviour.

Thus the essentials of marital counselling are listening to a couple describing how they feel about each other, what they want which is missing and how they see the future. Listening and clarifying, in order to help the couple identify and bring about the desired changes, is the essence of marital counselling.

Phases of counselling

These phases, described in a slim, easily readable book *Conversations on Counselling*, are here modified and set in the context of marriage counselling.

1. *Preparation*

Counselling requires the full attention of the counsellor. For an hour he is making his whole world, internal and external, available to the couple. He has to concentrate on what they are saying, make sense of it and convey this back to them. It is an undertaking which will not be based on extensive experience or marked familiarity. The counsellor will not be giving advice which he has given often before. Every couple present familiar problems but they are unique, and the preparation to meet their requirements must also be unique. The counsellor needs to approach the session free from immediate preoccupations which will intrude into the work of counselling. If he is distracted he will not receive fully the complexity of the situation. Instead he will convert the problem into a familiar and recognizable pattern with which he is acquainted, and he will apply preconceived, familiar, stereotype answers. Even the most skilled counsellors can fall into the trap of 'hearing' what they expect to hear and responding with standard, unoriginal observations. In this way couples can feel dismissed, treated as 'cases' and their uniqueness to be lost.

The counsellor needs to approach every couple in a completely fresh and open manner. He should empty himself of current preoccupations which will interfere with his attention. He needs to convey the feeling that he is experienced in the subject but is prepared to make a new journey with every couple and follow their particular signposts, discovering what is important to them. The approach to counselling needs to be that of a readiness to receive whatever is revealed and to treat it with skill, sensitivity, care and an original approach, so that no impression is given that the couple are the end-products of a factory process. Thus at the end of the session they should feel that it is *their* relationship that has been listened to, grasped and responded to accurately.

For all this to happen the counsellor must be truly available. The task of the session needs to be welcomed and the process must be free from interruptions, internal or external. All those who find themselves in need of counselling are basically deprived people. They feel that their spouse is unable to give them the minimum care, attention and understanding they need. Whatever help they may ultimately receive from counselling, they need to leave the session feeling cared for, attended to and understood.

2. *Listening, exploring and observing*

If the couple are to feel all this, it is necessary that they are carefully listened to. Listening is more than a matter of receiving words and construing their meaning. Not only must the counsellor listen fully but he also has to help the couple listen to each other. Listening in depth means hearing words, observing the manner of expression — for example, whether the words are accompanied by anger, pleasure, surprise, excitement, disbelief, sarcasm, rejection, concern, care or indifference. The ability to link words, sounds and feelings is called empathy. Each counsellor will have a variable ability to be empathetic, but empathy is a key element in counselling. Most of the time the couple are not empathetic towards each other. They listen without registering feelings and their associated messages. The counsellor has to register these feelings accurately and be able to show to the partners that they are angry, pleased, surprised, etc. with each other.

Listening and observing the couple helps the counsellor to appreciate feelings better. Who does the talking? With what degree of composure, violence, anxiety, tentativeness, detachment, indifference are they addressing each other? Observation also includes the way the couple relate to each other bodily. Do they look at each other when they are talking? Are their bodies relaxed? Do they wave their arms in various gestures? Are they tapping their feet angrily? A combination of listening and observing will reveal the emotional atmosphere, and at the appropriate moment the counsellor will comment on these feelings. Sometimes one or both of the couple are unaware what their feelings are. They may deny that they are feeling angry or any other emotion, and the counsellor has the task of helping them to recognize their unconscious or denied emotions. Sometimes spouses will learn, to their great surprise, from their partner what he or she is experiencing. The counselling session may reveal for the first time to a husband that his wife is angry, feels cut off, isolated, rejected, lonely, perhaps even desperate. The counsellor notes what the couple feel and, if they cannot appreciate this spontaneously, assists in its recognition at the appropriate moment.

Having discerned the emotional atmosphere, the counsellor must try to link feelings with events. What is causing these feelings? Is it their social, emotional, intellectual, spiritual life or their sexual relations? In the following four chapters these aspects of the relationship will be examined in detail. At this stage of listening the counsellor will receive the complaints of the partners. These may be numerous or small in number. Whatever their number, the counsellor has to recognize clearly which are central and which peripheral. The couple will talk about their social life in terms of not having enough time together, not going out, entertaining or having common interests. Still in the social sphere, they will commonly discuss money, helping with the household chores, looking after the children and maintaining the home. Emotionally, they will complain of too much criticism, too little affection, not enough understanding or communication. Sexually there will be complaints about too little or too much sex, poor love-making and sexual difficulties. Intellectually and spiritually there will be complaints about different values, opinions, outlook on life and lack of interest in each other's faith and practice.

The counsellor will either be bombarded with conflicts in all these areas or will have to elicit them by going through the relevant parameters of the relationship. Here lies the main difficulty. Whilst listening to all these complaints, he will have to be especially attentive to link the greatest distress with one or more particular complaint so that he can begin to form an order of priority in his mind. What is the greatest distress and with which aspect of the relationship is it linked? He will get some help in this from the couple who will emphasize those areas which distress them most either by signalling them with marked feelings or by repeating the same complaint at frequent intervals.

3. *Assimilation*

Whilst listening the counsellor is assimilating the infor-mation. He will interrupt when he needs to understand or clarify. He can intervene by saying, 'I am not sure what you mean. Can you tell me a little more, please?' or he may use the last sentence and repeat it, e.g. 'He always comes home late?' The repetition of a sentence usually causes further comments which clarify the meaning.

Having allowed the couple to exhaust spontaneously what they have to say to each other or by asking them specifically about the quality of their relationship socially, emotionally, sexually, intellectually and spiritually, the time has come for the counsellor to make a preliminary assessment of the main complaints and to summarize what he has heard. A summary is the best way of concluding the first part of the session. It allows the counsellor to assess whether he has heard them correctly and the couple to verify whether their point of view has been fully and accurately understood. The counsellor may say, 'Having listened to what you both have said, it seems to me that Jean feels angry with you, John, because you don't talk to her, never accept that you are in the wrong, are always criticizing her, and that you keep her short of money. You in turn, John, feel that your wife is not nice to you, is constantly complaining and is not interested in sex. That is how it comes across to me. Is that correct?' Such a formulation, or whatever is appropriate, tries to summarize the main feeling complaints linking them with the principal problems.

At this point the couple may agree with the summary and with each other that this is how the situation is, or agree with the summary but sternly deny that this is how they are behaving in practice and that their spouse's accusations are incorrect and unfair.

The counsellor then notes these differences and proceeds to clarify what is actually happening in practice. How often do they have sexual intercourse? How often does John talk to his wife? How much money does he give her? How often does Jean complain? Couples cannot resolve their difficulties because they are continually on the defensive and are not prepared to accept their spouse's criticism. The counsellor's task is to narrow gradually the areas of denial so that the couple can agree on what is actually happening in reality, instead of acting on imagination and phantasy. Recognizing reality is often difficult because the admission of certain behaviour may appear to be conceding defeat, to be accepting the grounds for the complaint. This is where counselling comes in with intervening help. 'I can see that you, John, find it difficult to accept what Jean is saying. As far as I am concerned Jean may be right or you may be right in protesting your innocence. The point that matters is that this is how Jean experiences you and you in turn experience Jean in this way. What counts is not so much what we do but how our partner receives it. Of course Jean may be right and you are doing this which annoys her. You are on the defensive because you feel that, if you agree, you will lay yourself open to be attacked, and criticized. As far as I am concerned, we are not here to pass judgement or attack each other. We are here to try to agree on what is actually happening, to find out why and to see whether we can change it.'

Slowly the counsellor is creating an atmosphere where attack, criticism and judgement are giving way to one in which the true situation can be admitted to without fear and without prejudicing one's standing *vis à vis* the partner. If Jean or John does admit to the criticized behaviour, the other may erupt in the following manner. 'I have been telling you this for years. It has needed us to come here for you to admit it. I told you what was wrong with you a long time ago. You are too selfish/lazy/self-centred to admit it.' John may retort with 'This is the trouble. If I agree to anything, I never hear the end of it. I can never do anything right. I know I'm not perfect, but Jean is never pleased with anything. Whatever I do is wrong, so I keep my mouth shut and don't say anything. I can never win an argument.'

Once again the counsellor has to intervene to save the situation which has become critical. Jean has been waiting a long time for justification. Her husband has admitted a weakness and there is a yell of triumph. The counsellor needs to come in. 'I know how you feel, Jean, you have been trying to tell your husband this for a very long time and now your chance has come. He has agreed to what you are saying, but you can see why he denied it all along and why he would not talk about it. As soon as he admits anything you are ready to attack him. So the only way for him to protect himself is by refusing to discuss the matter with you. He feels that whatever he says, he cannot please you. What is more, you are ready to jump in with moral judgements. In your eyes he is really bad. In fact whatever he does, he cannot please you. Instead of attacking him, we need to help him to find out why he cannot meet you, at least half-way, and if we are going to achieve this, he needs your understanding and help.'

It can be seen that the role of the counsellor at this stage is to go beyond the discharge of feelings, to help to lower the defences of the couple and to assist them to face honestly the reality of their mutual complaints. Once they agree on what are the real issues which make them unhappy, then both they and the counsellor can concentrate on trying to understand the underlying reasons and doing something about changing the situation.

4. *Diagnostic interlude*
The assimilation phase goes on until the couple can agree on what are their mutual complaints and the feelings associated with them. It is crucial for the counsellor to appreciate that when the session starts the spouses are armed with their complaints and criticism which they want to express, and

each wants to get him to side with them. The process of evaluation clarifies that both have complaints which need deeper understanding and that the counsellor is not taking sides with either partner. The essence of the evaluation is to help the spouses to realize that their complaints are unmet needs or unacceptable behaviour, which cannot be understood through adverse moral judgements and that more often than not both are contributing to the problem. When the complaint is entirely the aggression, alcoholism, or damaging behaviour of one partner, the victim finds it difficult to see how they are remotely responsible for the situation which exists. It is usually the wife who finds herself in this situation, and she gets angry when it is hinted that she has contributed to the difficulties. She may feel furious that the counsellor does not see the problem exclusively in terms of her husband's irresponsibility. The fact is, and this has to be pointed out, that for a long time she did nothing about the problem. Perhaps she was too frightened to say anything, or she hoped his behaviour would soon change. Whatever the reason she encouraged it by permitting it and not taking a strong enough stand against it.

By repeatedly summarizing the situation and getting the couple to agree with the formulation, the stage is reached when diagnosis comes into the counselling process. The diagnosis consists of agreeing what the problems are and then trying to understand them. The problems are usually narrowed down to two crucial issues, namely unmet needs and unacceptable behaviour. When there is agreement about these two points, counselling proceeds to discover the reasons for what is happening.

The simplest explanation is that the spouse concerned did not recognize their contribution to the problem and, having seen it for the first time, is now ready to alter their behaviour. In a few instances mutual alteration of behaviour will bring about the desired result. This is the happiest intervention of counselling and the dream of every counsellor, but alas it does not happen very often. Making available to one's partner what was absent before and changing behaviour which irritates often means three things. First it requires facing the underlying anxiety which has contributed to the behaviour. For example, the spouse who dominates is afraid of losing control, status, face and needs help to tackle these fears, to realize that his position in the family will not deteriorate if he stops dominating. The spouse who is constantly demanding attention needs to recognize their fears of being abandoned. Thus behind much behaviour lies a great deal of anxiety which has to be exposed.

Secondly, change requires acquiring a new repertoire of behaviour or the giving up of a particular practice. The way we behave is fashioned by our upbringing and/or our personality. A common complaint of wives is that their husband will not talk to them. A husband who wishes to please his wife must learn to handle both words and feelings, since these are the essentials of communication, and this acquisition does not come easily. It takes time and, what is more, requires the assistance of the wife, who rewards his efforts by appreciating them. One cannot emphasize too much that, when a spouse is trying to do something new which their partner wants, they need encouragement to achieve it. This encouragement is often not given because the deprived spouse expects them to change rapidly and without fuss. For them the change should have occurred a long time ago. They cannot appreciate what effort change requires, and so their partner gives up the attempt in despair. The same applies to the eradication of negative behaviour such as, for example, excessive criticism. Men and women who criticize all the time probably were at the receiving end of disapproval as children. They treat others as they were treated. Sometimes they were spoiled as children and they criticize their partner for not continuing the process. Whatever the reason, eradicating criticism takes sustained effort which once again requires encouragement, appreciation and reward.

Thirdly, the behaviour may be a deeply ingrained part of the personality. There is a widespread belief that some aspects of the personality do not alter, and much divorce takes place on the assumption that people cannot change. There is sufficient truth in this belief to make it part of the myths with which we conduct our lives, but this view is not entirely correct. There are aspects of the personality which can be modified. Thus we can shift from dependence to independence, from immature impulsive behaviour to more mature control of our impulses, from anxiety to confidence, from self-rejection to self-esteem and so on.

Having helped the couple to agree on the formulation of the problem by repeated summaries of the situation until they can accept most of the conclusions, the next step is to help them to see the reasons for their respective behaviour. These reasons have been summarized as excessive anxiety with its defences, childhood experiences and the personality. This is the diagnostic aspect of counselling, which the counsellor must gradually be doing as the counselling session unfolds. The diagnostic assessment may take one or more session to be completed and it is not as vital as the assessment of what the problems are. If the assessment is correct, the couple will leave the first session feeling understood in their immediate situation, and it is this which is vital.

But the diagnostic process has to go on, at least as far as the counsellor is concerned. He must assess what contributes to the behaviour and what are the chances of changing it. This assessment can be shared with the couple if they can make use of it. But some couples are not concerned with how their problems arose, all they want is change. This point is vital to counselling. A good deal of traditional counselling spends a lot of time helping the couple or the individual spouse to understand their childhood and the attitudes that spring from that phase in their life. In my opinion this can be helpful to some couples or individuals but it is often the reason why counselling is given up. What couples want is change in the here-and-now situation, and in my view this is best achieved by a minimum understanding of the past and a maximum change of current feelings and behaviour by conscious, deliberate alteration of behaviour which is rewarded by the spouse. Both in individual counselling and marital work, hours can be spent with the past at the expense of the present. Sometimes this is necessary, but usually it is the current situation that has the sense of urgency and needs focusing on. In technical terms there is a need to combine the dynamic, the world of feelings and emotions which arise from the past, with the behaviouristic approach, which concentrates on changing behaviour here and now by effort and reward. This change affects feelings as much as behaviour.

5. *Selection of a target*

Having listened to the problems and gradually proposed a formulation which is acceptable to the couple, the counsellor proceeds to work out with the couple what their immediate priorities are. There may be a single outstanding problem, in which case this becomes the sole target for change. But this does not often happen. The couple usually have problems in many areas. The counsellor has to dialogue with them regarding what is the most urgent matter in their lives. This may be simply to stop arguing. A truce can be declared until the next session, or the couple may need to go home and continue the discussion with the newly appreciated features which the counsellor has brought out. Whatever the priority is, the couple need to agree on what they want to happen next in their life. Often there are conflicting priorities, for example, over affection and sex. Sex will not be put right until the relation improves and so the target is to concentrate on these issues — be they social, emotional, intellectual or spiritual — which will enhance the relationship. Are questions about money, time spent listening to each other, time together, to have priority over having to express appreciation and be less critical? Are matters concerning the children to have priority over those that concern the couple, and in turn the issues of the relationship to come before the way the couple relate to their parents and relatives?

Everything cannot be tackled at once and there is a need to agree on those matters that cause the greatest havoc or can be changed most swiftly. The counsellor has to help the couple express their views about what they need most urgently and to examine the best way of achieving this. In practice most people want to feel loved, and the counsellor will keep in mind this universal need and try to encourage such change in behaviour which will give the couple the quickest feeling that their partner recognizes, wants and appreciates them. Some things hurt more than others and these need immediate attention.

6. *Working through the target areas*

Having decided what should be tackled first, the next question is how is this to be done? The very question may send shivers down the spine of some counsellors. We seem to be approaching the moment when the counsellor may have to give advice, whereas the essence of counselling is that it is not an advice-giving process. This is true but the matter is far more complex.

Most couples come to a counsellor because they have exhausted their own resources of how to resolve their problem. In fact they come for advice and they lay the trap at regular intervals during the session by asking, 'And how do we do that?' or, 'What do you think?' or, 'What would you do?' The trap for the counsellor is to use his own life experience, the commonsense he has acquired or simply give a rational reply in such terms, 'If I were you, I would do this,' or, 'Perhaps if you try this'. In fact often the couple have tried everything suggested and the advice is a waste of time. Maybe the advice is useful but it will only sort out this particular issue and very soon new problems will arise.

The essence of counselling is to help the couple recognize their problems, alter their understanding of the cause if inaccurate, if possible appreciate the origin of these difficulties in childhood and in the course of the marriage, and shift from an accusatory to a mutual understanding of what is happening. Whatever counselling theory may imply, the fact is that every counsellor does advise. But this advice should spring from the contents of the session. The advice is really the clarification and illumination of what has been discussed. It arises from the internal evidence of the session and is not an external intrusion of the counsellor. Thus advice is couched in terms of, 'It seems to me, from what we have been discussing that the issues are . . . and you need to discuss between yourselves the implications further'. Or, 'It seems to me that these are the problems and you need to go on talking about them'. Traditional counselling may summarize the issues but stops short of telling the couple that they need to discuss the matter further. In practice I find that this is unsatisfactory. If left to their own devices some couples will pursue the matter further, but others will leave the counsellor with one or the other saying, 'A waste of time . . . He didn't tell us what we should do'. Husbands in particular look for practical advice. As already mentioned, this advice is never the independent opinion of the counsellor of what should happen next. It must always follow the contents of the session and be directed at helping the couple understand them and their implications better.

In other instances however the advice is more direct. Once again arising entirely from the contents of the session and the agreement of the couple of what is needed, the directive is based on behaviouristic principles. Here the couple are advised to focus on one aspect of their behaviour and see how they can change this by modification and reward. This is nearer traditional advice but is far more sophisticated. The target for change is chosen by the couple and the counsellor. In its simplest form, the husband agrees to do something for his wife which she rewards by doing something for him in return, which he wants. This is mutual modification of behaviour by reinforcement through reward. At its crudest this might imply that the husband gives some money to his wife and she in return cooks for him dishes he enjoys. The possibilities of mutual rewarding are infinite and in fact operate in all marriages.

As already suggested, dynamic and behaviouristic counselling combine together. Through the counselling process a progressive clarification is reached of what the couple need from each other, and the feelings of satisfaction are linked with particular aspects of behaviour. At the dynamic or feeling level the object is to develop progressively mutual trust, security, acceptance, feelings of being wanted and appreciated. These feelings, which collectively contribute to the sense of being loved, are developed as behaviour changes and, as we have seen, behaviour changes by deliberate efforts which are appreciated and rewarded either in themselves or in kind.

Helping the couple into new life

Counselling can be short or last months and sometimes years. The counsellor remains available to facilitate the new style of life that is gradually evolving. He is there to inject hope, encouragement, share the joys of satisfactory change and the disappointment of failure or slow progress. An essential aspect of change is the need for a couple to be in tune with each other. Having brought their complaints out in the open, partners need to remain sympathetic to each other's efforts to change for the better. Sometimes a spouse has been burdened by so much pain, frustration and disappointment that their sense of hope, patience and encouragement is either non-existent or limited. If their resources of encouragement are totally depleted they do not have the patience to rekindle the relationship and the marriage breaks down. Some spouses are filled with hope after the first session and plunge into despair when things go wrong in the reconciliation. They lose hope quickly and return to violent criticism of the failure or poor progress of their partner.

The counsellor is there to remind couples that patience is needed, that there are no easy short cuts to reconstructing married life or indeed any life, that effort, perseverance and sacrifice are involved. The trouble is that so much pain has already been experienced that the thought of more is received with dread. In addition to offering patience, the counsellor is needed to spell out, to magnify small progress which is not recognized by the couple. A recurrent injection of hope, encouragement and appreciation of the effort made sustains the couple until they can see the progress themselves.

Further reading

On counselling:

M. Lefebure (ed.), *Conversations on Counselling.* T. and T. Clark, Edinburgh, 1982.
F. Kennedy, *On Being a Counsellor.* Gill and MacMillan, Dublin, 1977.
G. Egan, *The Skilled Helper; a Model for Systematic Helping and Interpersonal Relating.* Brooks Cole, California, 1975.

Philosophy of counselling:

P. Halmos, *The Faith of the Counsellor.* Constable, 1965.

General:

J. Dominian, *Marital Breakdown.* Penguin, 1968.

SEVEN

In the Counselling Room

The counselling situation

Traditionally counselling has taken place in the office of the counselling service and not in the home of the couple. The counsellor does well to insist on seeing the couple in a venue other than their house. It may be his own place or office. This does require that every time the couple come they exercise their free choice to participate or not. It means that effort is expended in attending, which shows their motivation. Above all it recognizes that a problem exists which needs resolution. If the counsellor comes to their home, he may be intruding, or appear to insist that there is a difficulty which one or other partner does not admit.

Counselling should take place in comfortable surroundings with three chairs placed so that the couple sit next to each other and the counsellor sits facing them. There should be no interruptions from telephone calls, and the time allocated, usually between 60 and 90 minutes, should be strictly adhered to.

When the couple are comfortably seated, the counsellor should introduce himself, if unknown to either partner. He should decide whether the contents of the interview will be taken down whilst it is proceeding, recorded on tape, or a summary transcribed at the end. It is helpful to keep a full and accurate record of each session and I prefer to take notes whilst the couple are talking.

With a pad on one's knees, the counsellor starts. 'I understand you have come to see me because you are experiencing difficulties in your marriage. In a moment we shall go into these, but before doing this can you tell me your age, how long you have been married, how many children you have, their ages and whether this is the first or second marriage.' All this is noted down and then he says, 'Now please tell me about your difficulties'. He notes whether it is the husband or wife who starts and how the conversation goes. It is essential to interrupt as little as possible, except for clarification, until the couple have exhausted their story.

From the schema I shall present in the next few chapters, it will be seen that five dimensions, or parameters, of the marriage relationship cover its main aspects. These are the emotional, sexual, social, intellectual and spiritual features. In the course of listening to the story it is important to keep these in mind and to assess whether they have been covered, at least minimally, in the account given. If one dimension has been left out, it can be added by questioning when the couple have finished their story.

Sometimes a couple do not know how to start or even what to say. The five parameters can help the counsellor to ask the relevant questions. The counsellor can start by saying, 'Many marriages run into difficulties because affection is missing in their relationship. How are things with you two?' Once a couple start talking, they move from topic to topic with greater ease. As soon as they can express their views spontaneously, the counsellor ceases asking questions and reverts to listening, but always making sure that the five areas have been covered.

When the story has been completed the counsellor can proceed to ask a little about each partner's background. The essentials to be noted are whether the parents are alive, how old they are, and what was the relationship of each spouse to their parents and brothers or sisters in childhood. This information gives essential knowledge about childhood experiences which are so relevant to the development of feelings and attitues.

In particular the type of relationship each spouse had with their parents should be noted. Did they lose them when young? Did the parents split up? Did they feel secure in the surroundings in which they were brought up? Did they live with feelings of being unwanted, rejected, criticized or with the fear of being abandoned by mother or father? Did they feel their parents preferred a brother or sister? Often the couple will speak spontaneously about their childhood experiences, or they may need specific probing. Either way the relationship with parents is the first intimate experience of love in life and is often repeated in the second experience in marriage. This is the important link between childhood and marriage and this connection is vital in appreciating the marital relationship.

The essentials of history-taking are thus reduced to three. At the outset, the age of the couple, the duration of marriage, whether it is the first or subsequent, the size of the family and the work done by one or both are noted. This is followed by the spontaneous or assisted unfolding of the story and finally the childhood experiences are identified.

It is at this stage that the first summary is attempted, which is then refined as the session proceeds. This summary is a combination of the principal features of the complaints and, as the session continues, it is filled up at the diagnostic level with the contribution of childhood. These abbreviated formulations should also be transcribed in the notes with the initials of the counsellor against them, so that the summary of the exchange is as comprehensive as possible.

At the end of the session it is vital that the couple are left with a formulation of their problems which makes some sense to them and a plan to proceed with in the interval until they are seen again. Some counsellors make the diagnostic formulation and say no more, leaving the actual programme to the couple themselves. This is the orthodox and classical approach in which the counsellor clarifies but does not advise. In the previous chapter this matter was discussed. In my own practice I like to help the couple to understand the next step, which may involve further discussion between themselves, or an active behaviour programme or both. I recognize that my medical training influences my practice, but I am very conscious of the fact that the open-ended conclusion of the first session leaves many couples confused and they simply do not return.

Towards the end of the session the counsellor has to assess when the couple need to be seen again. This can be after one, two, three or more weeks. An average of one or two weeks initially is the appropriate interval of sessions.

At the next session the original structure is repeated with an opening remark such as, 'It is two weeks since I saw you here last. Please tell me how things are now?' The counsellor listens to what has happened, particularly to fresh material and, noting all this, reformulates the situation, sets new targets and intervenes with the appropriate encouragement, appreciation of effort and injection of hope. Sessions continue until the couple can be left safely on their own or they cease coming.

Reconciliation or separation

Counselling is not a process which guarantees reconciliation. That is a highly desirable outcome and every effort is made to achieve this, but couples may come to a counsellor at a stage of irretrievable breakdown of the relationship. In the course of counselling it becomes abundantly clear that either no relationship ever existed or none exists currently. It is not the counsellor's task to tell or recommend couples to separate, in fact he must never do so. This is a decision for the couple and for the couple alone, but the counsellor can, through clarification, show the absence of any viable relationship if this is the case. Thus couples may come to a counsellor only to discover clearly what they already feared, that no relationship exists, in which case counselling may in fact act as a catalyst and bring about a separation long overdue.

Sometimes the counsellor may recognize very early on that a marriage is in a most precarious situation and that it is only continuing because one spouse is afraid to leave. The instability of the situation is revealed by the fact that one or both partners have ceased to love one another, have no sexual life and do not want one, but are staying together through habit, out of fear, for the sake of the children or through a lack of drive to take action. Counselling shows clearly the hopelessness of the situation, and one spouse gathers the encouragement and strength, through the counsellor, to take action. As soon as the counsellor recognizes the possibility of this outcome, he must inform the couple of this, so that they appreciate the alternatives that counselling may bring about. This is particularly the case in those marriages when a spouse, often the wife, has ceased to love but is dependent on her husband. This dependence can be transferred to the counsellor who may give her the necessary encouragement to become independent and find the strength to leave.

This possibility leads to an important aspect of counselling.

The counsellor must try to remain as impartial as possible. Sometimes however he may develop a strong sympathy for one partner and shows this by the way he is handling the summary of the problem. This is a danger which the counsellor has to guard against, but in any case he must recognize its occurrence and consciously correct the situation. One of the reasons for a married couple undertaking counselling with two counsellors is to guard against such biases.

Counselling and the sexes

The reader may have already noted that the examples given in this and the previous chapter have focused on the problems wives present. This has been done deliberately. There is considerable evidence that wives become aware of marital problems before their husbands, wish to correct them at an earlier stage than their spouses, seek help more often than men and are much more ready to disclose and discuss the issues that concern them. In brief the husband takes longer to recognize and accept that there is a problem and is often unwilling to seek help. This means that in practice it is the wife who often takes the first step in seeking help, and the challenge is to get the husband to co-operate. This can be done by writing to invite him to present his side of the story, by making it clear that counselling is not a court procedure and by indicating clearly that the counsellor is perfectly well aware that marital problems are the result of the actions of two people, both of whom need to examine their position. At the practical level the husband is invited to participate on the basis that there are always two sides to a problem and both need to be heard and attended to.

During counselling men find it difficult to appreciate the feeling side of the relationship, which is precisely what their wives wish to concentrate on. A vital part of counselling is that the counsellor is aware of this feeling dimension and helps the man to recognize it as fully as possible. Men often escape from their feelings by dismissing them as unmanly and belonging to women only. In fact husbands want as much love as their wives, only they recognize it more often in practical experiences of care such as food and sex. They love back by earning money, doing things in the home and generally adopting the role of providers. During counselling men will excuse themselves from talking, communicating, listening, spending time together with their family, because, having done their work, they are too tired to do anything else. There is always some truth in this declaration but often behind the objective situation lies a marked inability to talk, listen, exchange feelings and share. One of the constant complaints of wives is that husbands come home from work, have their meal, watch television and are totally unwilling to discuss anything of importance. The defence of the husbands is tiredness, but in fact they cannot discuss anything of substance at weekends either, so that an excuse of tiredness has a ring of hollowness about it. The counsellor should not be afraid to point out this deficiency and indicate that effort and persistence are needed to overcome it.

When men do come they often want to transform the nature of counselling and to reduce it to practical matters. Finding feelings difficult, they want to be told what to do and the counsellor to tell their wife how to behave. If the counsellor persists in looking at feelings, they get a sense of frustration with the session and tend to withdraw. When both spouses find feeling inter-action difficult, the counselling may be directed entirely on behaviouristic principles in which the couple are encouraged to change behaviour by rewarding each other with appropriate action which is desired by the partner.

Another feature which distinguishes male and female reaction in marriage is the fact that wives often get tense and depressed by the persistence of marital problems. Their husbands, wishing to avoid looking at the issues, hide behind their wives' illness and pretend that the whole matter rests with her and it will be resolved when she gets better. Sometimes the wife does not recognize that her symptoms spring from the marital conflict and begins seriously to question her sanity. This self-doubt is not assisted if the husband accuses her of being mad or hysterical as she gives way to crying, shouting and behaving in a disturbed way. It is vital that the counsellor who sees the wife alone does not fall into the trap of siding with the husband and reaching the conclusion that the whole problem would be resolved if the wife recovered. In fact the counsellor must be clearly on his guard against such explanations and realize that the husband is contributing to the ill health of his wife.

Counselling and socio-economic groups

The vast majority of counselling takes place with those men and women who are capable of articulating their thoughts and feelings, and these are the minority of people in the upper socio-economic groups. This does not imply that the lower socio-economic groups of people do not have feelings. Feelings exist in all groups. What differentiates them is the ability to articulate. Nevertheless counselling can be carried out with any couple, however impoverished they may be in language, provided that they can recognize the feeling issues.

There is however a tendency for the lower socio-economic groups to associate feelings with practical and material issues. Money, housing, possessions, work are often the controversial factors in these families, and it is these matters that are associated with conflict. The problems here are often the poor providing ability of the husband or the limited management capacity of the wife. In these circumstances counselling may need a close alliance with practical help.

Counselling one partner

The ideal, set out in this book, is that counselling should take place with a couple. Reasons have already been given why this may not always be possible. Often the husband will not participate or he withdraws after a few sessions. More rarely it is the wife who does not wish to be involved.

In these situations counselling can continue with one partner. She is helped to see the partner's point of view in his absence, is encouraged to avoid behaviour which is provocative or which aggravates the situation and also is assisted to be more helpful and encouraging. A good deal can be achieved in this way.

Sometimes the assistance given to one partner actually leads to their departure from the matrimonial home. In the course of counselling they have come to see that they are not mad or bad, and that all the things their spouse has blamed them for are not true. Gradually they lose the sense of guilt that the matrimonial difficulties are solely their fault. They appreciate that some of the problems belong to their spouse who is confronted for the first time. This confrontation may yield positive results or may not be productive. Having realized that the marital situation is not entirely their own doing, they may also gradually find they have more strength to survive than they imagined they had. A combination of a rise in self-esteem and freedom from guilt may be sufficient to extricate them from a dependent relationship. The counsellor plays a prominent part in this process.

Counselling however may also be needed when one spouse is abandoned by their partner who departs suddenly. The one who is left behind is often in a state of shock. They do not know or understand why their partner has left them. They are hurt, depressed and angry. The counsellor may attempt to bring the partners together again and try counselling. If this fails, the abandoned partner needs support to cope with the sense of loss and the anger associated with it. The sense of loss may only last for weeks but it can extend for months or even years.

Referral to another agency

Everyone is a potential counsellor because couples or individual partners come to any one of us for help and advice. It is essential that the initial response should be sufficiently helpful and accurate to give them some authentic insight into the marital conflict which is facing them. So much of the so-called 'common-sense' approach to marital problems is seriously limited by the individual's own life experience and marital background. Real help comes with the expansion of understanding which goes beyond these elements to the point of appreciating as accurately as possible the reality which afflicts the specific marriage in distress. Only then is there any hope of intervening effectively.

So everyone should be familiar with an outline of current understanding of marital problems in order to give first aid. In this way everyone is a potential counsellor, but clearly some people are more suited than others to undertake extensive counselling. Anyone who finds themselves in a situation, where they have undertaken counselling in its initial stages and then problems arise which are beyond their capacity to cope with, should feel free to suggest to a couple that they seek more expert help. This help can involve further marital counselling or assistance with sexual problems. The counsellor who refers a couple or an individual for more expert help should not do so with any sense of failure. Their task is to persuade a couple that they have problems which need more help than he can offer. It should be stressed that in no sense is this an abandonment and there should be an associated offer that they can always return to him if they wish.

The minister who finds himself involved in continuous counselling of a couple may find he needs to discuss what he is doing with someone more experienced. It is important for those who undertake more prolonged counselling to find a supervisor. Such a person may be found from the local marriage guidance council or from the ranks of those with experience in general counselling.

Further reading

J. Brannen and J. Collard, *Marriages in Trouble.* Tavistock Publications, 1982.

EIGHT

Phases of Marriage

It will be clear by now that traditional marital counselling has concentrated on understanding the development of the personality particularly in dynamic terms, i.e. the relationship of the individuals with their parents, leading to the dynamic interaction of the couple. Understanding the growth of the personality means that basic needs which amount to the sense of being loved are recognized. Interaction with parents helps us to appreciate how these needs of love were met in childhood and were either dealt with adequately or distorted. Finally the combination of these two factors are examined in the current needs of love of a couple in their marriage and how they are satisfied, distorted or denied.

Most counselling proceeds along these lines and of course there is a great deal of validity in this approach. In practice a good deal of marital conflict is related to the absence of loving feelings, and the appreciation of dynamic or feeling factors is of the greatest importance. But the absence of love in marriage is experienced in more than one dimension and the needs of a couple change with time.

With these considerations in mind I have pioneered a slightly different approach to marriage counselling. In it feelings remain crucial but much more is taken into account.

The two factors that are considered are the needs of the couple and the phase the marriage is in.

The five dimensions of marriage

A couple relate to each other on the basis of five dimensions. These are social, emotional, sexual, intellectual and spiritual. In this schema the encounter of spouses is extended to cover the five essential areas within which they discover themselves and each other as significant people. If a marriage is to survive it must be viable in at least one of these dimensions and usually in more than one.

1. *The social dimension*

When a couple decide to marry they need to find accommodation, set up a home (if they are fortunate enough to obtain a separate dwelling), agree between themselves their respective responsibilities, the place of work and how to handle their finances.

All this is dealt with within a social framework of the respective roles and relationship between men and women. These vary between different societies and within the same society. In particular, women are emerging from a position of inferiority to that of equality, and the implications of this change are monumental.

The social life of the couple in their home is intimately related to their outer life in terms of the social network to which they belong. Spouses leave families of origin, relatives, friends and form a new unit. Hence the couple, which form the new unit, have to relate to and attempt to harmonize their availability to their own and their spouse's social network.

Finally, a couple form a social world of their own with their children, new friends and acquaintances. This new social world will make demands on their time which will be divided between work, home, periods of exclusive togetherness and socializing. Everyone knows that a good deal of marital conflict is associated with all these social factors, which must be assessed in counselling.

2. *The intellectual dimension*

Spouses come to each other usually from similar social and educational backgrounds, but even so their gifts, talents and intellectual skills may vary. One spouse may have practical aptitudes, another artistic and creative, yet another the ability to relate well with people. Within strictly equivalent intelligences men and women may enjoy different hobbies, including music, drama, sport, gardening, walking, crafts, etc. All these differences usually mean an enrichment of the relationship when this is harmonious. When it is not, the complaint is that spouses have nothing in common. Furthermore the way they approach problems may vary.

3. *The spiritual dimension*

Even in a secular age like ours some 20 per cent of society attend church regularly, and religion remains important for many more. Thus for numerous couples church attendance, the religious education of children and indirectly such matters as contraception, abortion, divorce are of crucial significance.

But even when couples do not have such overt faith their life is controlled by important values. There may be a clash of values, and often this is related to the priority that one spouse gives to material matters such as money, property, wealth, status, power and position as against those of their partner who is interested in the life of the home, having time together and for the children. There may be clashes about the education of the children and, in these difficult times, about moral values.

4. *The sexual dimension*

A central element of the marriage relationship is its sexual life. Nowadays the sexual dimension has assumed an ever increasing significance and couples are acutely aware when sex is missing from their life. Thus the frequency and quality of sexual intercourse is a vital element in the marital relationship and it represents a powerful expression of love.

5. *The emotional dimension*

Traditionally marriage counselling concentrates on the emotional side of marriage which is the world of feelings that spell out love or hate. Spouses need to feel recognized, wanted and appreciated by each other. This often means a minimum of physical closeness, time together, signals of affirmation, not too much criticism or rejection, reasonable communication and a sense of belonging and being needed. These are the means by which the couple feel they have meaning for each other. But ultimately the emotional dimension includes all the other aspects of behaviour. If any one of these is seriously defective or causing conflict, then the emotional side suffers and, when couples say they do not love each other any more, it often means that the emotional language of love reflects the gradual impoverishment in all the other areas.

Timing

These five dimensions are important throughout marriage, but their significance varies and so does their character. For example the absence of the sexual relations matters a great deal more at the beginning of marriage than after thirty or forty years of married life when affection can be experienced in other ways, even though sex remains important far longer than it used to be.

Change is of the very essence of marriage, something which was poorly grasped when matrimony was considered primarily as a fixed contract. Nowadays when marriage is seen far more as a relationship which extends and unfolds over many decades, what is happening during its different periods is of the greatest importance to its integrity.

Phases in marriage

The concept of phases in marriage is a sociological one and derives from American sources. The author has adapted it to three phases.

The first five years (First Phase)
The average age for marriage in the United Kingdom is about 25 for men and 23 for women. Thus the first five years of marriage take it to the later twenties or to the age of 30. This is the first phase and its duration is not an arbitrary decision. There is good evidence to suggest that these five years are crucial. Some 30—40 per cent of all marital breakdown occurs during these years; whenever marriage breaks up, some 50 per cent of the causes arise in this phase.

It is the phase when the marital relationship is established. Breakdown often means that the relationship has never got off the ground. Despite external appearances to the contrary, the internal relationship has not reached a minimum degree of cohesion. These early years are crucial and need a great deal of support.

Age 30 to 50 (Second phase)
This is the period when the children are growing up, and

towards the end of this phase they are ready to leave home or have already left it. Fifty is also the average age of the menopause of women and the termination of their reproductive years. Thus these two decades are often taken up with the life of the children.

Children have a powerful impact on marriage, but something else is of equal importance during this second phase. These are the years when men and women change. This change is in all the dimensions mentioned and can be dramatic. Essentially the spouses find out their authentic sense of self. They are no longer prepared to relate out of fear, duty or simply to please. There is a gradual emergence of the real person who finds that they have shed their fears, doubts and uncertainties and are more clear and precise as to who they are and what they want of life. Such changes may have dramatic consequences for marriage, for a spouse may find that their newly discovered self has no basic connection with their partner, who then becomes irrelevant in their life.

Much conflict during these years springs from the gradual changes in the personality of the spouses and the need for renewed adaptation at fresh levels of interaction.

From age 50 to death (Third phase)

This third and final phase is a recent addition to marriage within Western society. It is during this century that the average span of life has reached the seventies, and so another twenty years have been added to the duration of marriage. During the early part of this period, immediately after the children depart, there is another upsurge of marital breakdown. Normally however this is a time of fulfilment.

Implementation of the schema

The schema outlined here has certain advantages. It is a far more comprehensive study of the totality of marriage. Given that most couples reach the marriage counsellor with emotional conflict, this schema allows the greatest possible basis for understanding what contributes to it. For many couples who find an exclusively dynamic approach to their problems difficult this schema allows a wider understanding of their particular problems.

As far as the counsellor is concerned, this schema allows him to inquire widely about the marriage and to assess what are the principal problems. Furthermore, even before the story is given, the basic facts about the duration of the marriage allows him to focus with particular emphasis on the points in the relationship which are likely to be of significance so that he is not exploring in the dark. With a little experience, patterns of marital problems begin to emerge which are recognizable and which give the counsellor a sense of confidence which he can share with the couple, that the problems may be difficult to negotiate but they are not all that mysterious. Often couples ask whether their problems are unique and it is most reassuring for them to realize that this is not the case.

Further reading

S. Bloch (ed.), *An Introduction to the Psychotherapies.* Oxford University Press, 1979.

J. Bowlby, *The Making and Breaking of Affectional Bonds.* Tavistock Publications, 1979.

H. V. Dicks, *Marital Tensions.* Routledge and Kegan Paul, 1967.

E. M. Duvall, *Marriage and Family Development.* J. B. Lippincott, Philadelphia, 1977.

T. J. Paolino and B. S. McGrady, *Marriage and Marital Therapy: Psychoanalytic, Behavioural and Systems Theory Perspectives.* Brunner Mazel, New York, 1976.

A. C. R. Skynner, *One Flesh, Separate Persons.* Constable, 1976.

NINE

First Phase: The Early Years

The early years of marriage are crucial in three respects. A very small number of people take flight from the relationship within a short time. Spouses may find that their partner abandons them on their honeymoon, or after a few weeks or months of marriage. Such men and women find that the relationship is impossible for them, panic and depart suddenly and impulsively.

A larger number stay for longer periods, perhaps one year or more, and then they depart, sometimes abandoning very young children. These men and women come to the conclusion consciously and clearly that the relationship is not viable or reach the same decision intuitively, and also depart. As already mentioned some 30—40 per cent of marriages end effectively in these first five years.

Finally, at whatever stage marriages break down, some 50 per cent of the problems which lead to the termination emerge within five years, with the first year being prominent in unveiling the principal conflict.

In this first phase, as at any time, a couple will run into serious difficulties when they feel unloved, a feeling which will arise from an insufficient level of satisfaction in one or more of the five dimensions. Every spouse will appreciate the five dimensions differently depending on their needs, expectations and experiences. The order of presentation here is not meant to indicate any priority of significance. Whatever the difficulty, its meaning will ultimately be conveyed through feeling unloved. In turn this will be experienced in terms of security (material or emotional), significance (that is, feeling recognized, wanted and appreciated) and belonging (which implies that one has relevance for the spouse). Problems may exist which can be tolerated in one marriage and not in another. Tolerance to a problem will depend on the resources of the spouses, but when breakdown occurs in these early years, it often suggests that one or both spouses have very little strength and the slightest degree of turmoil is enough to tip the balance in favour of dissolution.

1. The social dimension

(a) Parental Separation

As already mentioned marriage means separating from one's family or origin and forming a new social unit. This means in practice that spouses remain in friendly relations with their parents, brothers and sisters but regard their spouse as the principal figure of significance in their life. It is with the husband or wife that the main communication takes place about those matters which concern their life, the running of the home and the care of their children. This also means that the spouse is treated as the principal confidante. This new channel of communication does not exclude discussion with parents but it does mean that the spouse's views, wishes and preferences receive special attention. Spouses are not locked in an exclusive world, but their inner world has priority.

There are a number of difficulties which arise from this social merging. Sometimes parents strongly disapprove of their future son- or daughter-in-law and may even absent themselves from the wedding ceremony. Often this initial negation is gradually softened, particularly when grand-children arrive. But when it persists it is associated with a high incidence of marital breakdown, which may be linked with the absence of support a young couple usually receive from their parents.

The assistance that parents give to their children varies. Sometimes it is financial or material but often it is continuous encouragement and help. Such assistance is often stronger between mother and daughter than father and son, so that the maintenance of a good relationship between the two women is of particular value, provided that the husband does not feel bypassed.

Difficulties exist when a spouse remains socially and emotionally over-attached to either parent after marriage. Thus the husband who insists on visiting his parents every day or weekly and sacrifices his spare time with his wife and family may cause annoyance. The wife who insists on visiting her mother daily, taking advice from her, confiding to her the couple's secrets, angers the husband who feels that he is ignored and cannot trust his wife.

Sometimes both spouses find it impossible to escape from their family of origin and are constantly arguing who they should visit or listen to in important matters.

In all these instances one spouse may feel rejected and the other feel placed in a situation of divided loyalty, having to respond to competing priorities between partner and parent.

Having identified this problem, the couple need to be helped with several factors. The continuous attachment to the parent may be merely habit, it may express unrecognized anxiety about trusting the spouse or it may reflect the pressure the parent is putting on their child not to abandon them. All these points need examination. Does the spouse really recognize that they are bypassing their partner? It is even more difficult to appreciate that the anxiety that pressurizes them to confide in their parent is because they do not trust their spouse. This last reason is hard to admit, but it has to be faced, and the mistrusted partner needs to become a secure person for their spouse. Finally the anxiety of the parent, who may feel abandoned, needs to be taken into consideration. Do they have to be visited daily? Weekly? Can they be telephoned instead? Do they need to be rung daily? The easing of all these problems is likely to occur only when the underlying anxiety and guilt is reduced.

Sometimes, another problem features. In this situation both spouses decide to repudiate their family. They marry, cling to each other and ignore their parents. It is a way of asserting their independence. This works out if both are ready to sever their emotional ties and can find in each other the strength and security they need. But problems arise when either or both feel guilty about distancing themselves from their parents. Feelings of guilt may have the powerful effect of mobilizing anxiety and/or depression, which makes the spouse irritable and in turn renders the marital relationship stormy. The discontent may be accentuated by the fact that independence from parents usually means reliance on the partner. If the partner has not got the resources to shoulder this, then the emancipating spouse feels both the guilt of separation and the anxiety of insecurity. When both partners are emancipating but neither can meet the other's needs, the marriage is in deep disarray. Here counselling is needed for both partners individually so that their needs are met and their resources enhanced.

Of course these marriages are fragile because what unites the couple is their determination to separate from homes where they felt suffocated and whose values they repudiate. The determining factor is the seeking of personal emancipation. It may be that beyond this common goal there is enough similarity and common purpose to keep the marriage afloat, but often such unions have very little in common, other than the desire to escape the parental atmosphere. When this has been achieved, they discover that what holds them together is very limited and the marriage breaks down, sometimes to the delight of the parents who are eagerly awaiting the return of their escapee.

(b) Housing

In our society most newly married couples desire their own home. This is a hope much more likely to be realized in the early years by the upper socio-economic groups. Others have to share with parents, in-laws or friends. This sharing may work out satisfactorily but it may lead to arguments and even quarrels. The newly married wife may be at a disadvantage *vis-à-vis* her mother or mother-in-law in being allowed to do things her way in the kitchen or elsewhere. She may be sensitive about privacy and find making love in a house with thin walls difficult. If there are children, grandparents may interfere with their upbringing and in general the independence of the couple is threatened.

Housing may be even more difficult than this, and a couple unable to share with relatives may have to move frequently, which is unsatisfactory.

In these constrained situations the early years of marriage are afflicted by a social handicap which may have emotional overtones. The couple may accept their financial limitations, but sometimes the wife feels annoyed that her husband is not a better provider. The husband's self-esteem may suffer, and the level of stress, elevated by the confined circumstances and emotional conflict, causes quarrels which embitter the relationship early on.

(c) Household management

When accommodation has been obtained, the couple have to establish their respective roles and their mutual responsibilities. Traditionally wives looked after the home whilst their husbands went out to work and acted primarily as providers. The current situation is much more fluid and both sexes undertake tasks which belonged exclusively to the other in the past. Thus husbands help in the home and wives go out to work. The actual distribution of responsibility is something the couple will decide between themselves. Nowadays some husbands cook, wash up, clean the house, shop and undertake many traditional feminine tasks.

Problems arise when, before marriage, a husband has promised, or suggested, that he would be responsible for tasks which he does not then carry out in practice. Since the wife often works at the start of the marriage, she finds herself in a situation, saddled both with work and the whole responsibility of the household chores. This may result in her feeling excessively tired, even betrayed, and leads to frustrated anger. Fatigue may in fact inhibit her sexually, and the marriage starts with marked dissatisfaction.

Another feature which appears frequently in marital conflict is the husband who accepts responsibility for practical matters and will enthusiastically begin to alter the kitchen or other rooms, put up cupboards, redecorate, build furniture, or even attempt to modify the house in some radical way. The characteristic complaint is that he never finishes what he starts or that completion may be prolonged over weeks, months and sometimes years, having sometimes to be finished by the wife. The distress and annoyance over the incomplete project is often made worse by the fact that during this same period, when no progress is made at home, he will do things willingly and successfully for other people. The wife becomes really angry that her needs have been ignored and often others are put before her.

When the husband is confronted with this accusation he may have no excuses, but gentle prodding may reveal several psychological reasons. He may have the sort of personality that starts things with enthusiasm but finds it difficult to finish them. Such people need a lot of encouragement to complete their task. Often they need their wife to appreciate their handiwork at regular intervals in a way which urges them to finish it. They get easily discouraged and need, as young children do, constant reassurance that they are on the right lines. Sometimes these men find it difficult to work alone and the job is finished rapidly when the wife offers to participate. Some men will excuse themselves with the explanation that they have stopped working or do not undertake new ventures because whatever they do does not please their wife. Indeed the wife may be over-critical or unappreciative of their achievements, being concerned only with the fact that they are continuously busy on her behalf.

The complaint that the husband promises and completes tasks for others whilst leaving those of his home undone is often true. This grumble is linked with several others. He is criticized for saying 'Yes' to others and constantly 'No' to his wife, for rarely disagreeing with others whilst always doing so with her, for being eager to please others whilst indifferent to her needs. Such a constellation of behaviour often suggests a man who is diffident, anxious, unsure of himself, frightened to contradict and is for ever trying to please, appease and win approval from others, whilst home is the only place where he finds the confidence to be himself. In trying to ingratiate himself with others, such a person amasses a lot of anger and frustration, which he displaces at home—his wife being the recipient of these, possibly unconscious, factors.

(d) Money

Money is a source of frequent complaints. It has two distinct meanings. Firstly it has economic significance. A spouse, often the wife, may be kept short of sufficient money to run the home and maintain herself and the children. So unravelling the actual financial details is important in making some objective assessment of the complaint. There are husbands who are really generous, married to wives who have impossible expectations or who find it impossible to manage. Often however the husband lives in a world of economic phantasy in which he expects his wife to cope with allowances which are clearly insufficient. Secondly, money has an emotional meaning. When a spouse is kept short of money or it is procured with difficulty, a feeling of being financially ignored amounts to being emotionally neglected as well.

At the start of marriage both spouses are likely to be working and two issues have to be settled, namely how the money is handled and how it is used. Couples may decide to have a joint account from which they draw according to their needs, having decided their respective financial responsibilities. Often the husband pays the bills, including the mortgage, and the wife buys food. On other occasions the couple retain separate accounts but also have a joint one. The separate accounts are used for their private needs and savings and the joint account for their mutual responsibilities for running the home. On other occasions only separate accounts are kept.

The presence of a joint account usually means that spouses know what they earn, have in common, and their current monthly situation. Later on there is unlikely to be a complaint that they are not aware of their spouse's income, have no idea of the family's resources and have been kept in the dark about the financial position.

Complaints about money emerge later in the marriage, but their origins are to be found in the way the foundations are laid in these early years.

The existence of separate accounts, particularly for the wife, may be important for some women who need to experience some degree of independence from their husband. When they are working they feel they have money of their own which they can handle as they wish, spend or save. When they cease to work, they may have an allowance which they can call their own. For some wives however an allowance is still linked with a feeling of social and emotional dependence on their husband and they are only satisfied when they are working and have money of their own.

Bank accounts are becoming increasingly common but a lot of couples are still paid through wage packets. The same principles apply. The wife needs to feel that she is getting enough money to make ends meet and, when she is working, that her husband does not keep her short of money which has then to be made up by her contribution. A combination of sufficiency for needs, preservation of economic independence wherever possible and a degree of generosity contributes to financial peace and contentment. Problems abound when the wife is kept short, given no independence, her competence doubted, or when the husband constantly grumbles when he is asked for money.

But more serious problems exist when one spouse, often the husband, is financially irresponsible. Such a man spends money impulsively, more than he earns and keeps his wife short or, when she is working, uses her resources for his purposes. In addition such a husband may be unable to cope with bills, which are left unpaid until sometimes essential supplies are cut off. In these instances the wife may have to step in and take over total responsibility for financial matters. This problem can be reversed and in some instances it is the wife who is incapable of managing money and the husband who has to intervene.

Occasionally the difficulty is less acute but no less real, as when one partner is much more carefree with money than the other and is in fact impulsive and spendthrift. Such a combination is often associated with much conflict. The person who is careful to the point of appearing stingy is often one whose anxiety rises at the thought of being left penniless or financially insecure. The fuss they make is linked with the degree of anxiety which threatens the state of impecuniousness. This anxiety clashes with the attitude of the partner who does not value money in the same way, does not feel anxious about having little of it, remains optimistic that resources will be found and is not threatened by financial matters.

If we look carefully at the childhood of the withholding person, we may find the presence of poverty, deprivation and a struggle to overcome financial adversity. Such a childhood may have instilled deep feelings of caution and a fierce desire never to find oneself in similar circumstances. This is an obvious explanation of the attitude of careful people in financial matters. But the financially anxious person may not have had such a background at all; he may experience anxiety over money as part of the overall anxiety and insecurity in his life. A sense of insecurity in childhood, expressed particularly in a feeling about inept parents or a father who could not look after the family properly, may lead to a determination never to find oneself in similar circumstances. Money is also linked with power, and the person who enjoys power from a sense of insecurity, in order to prove himself or as a means of controlling others, holds on to money in a very tenacious way because it becomes the sole way of feeling important.

Thus conflict over money uncovers many aspects of the personality linked with childhood experiences or with constitutional aspects of the personality such as rigidity, anxiety and obsessionality. The desire to make, retain and control money originates, in Freudian theory, with the child's earliest possession, namely faeces, which are made, retained or released and are a means of resistance over the power which mother possesses. This symbolism may or may not be true but it indicates the deep connection between personality and money and its extensive importance in the marital relationship.

(e) Work

Money and work are closely connected. At the beginning of the marriage both spouses are likely to be employed. At least, this was largely true until recently, before unemployment began to rise. It is still likely to be true in the majority of marriages and this means that money will not be short at this early stage. Work for the husband is accepted widely by society as a norm and does not lead to conflict. However, conflict may arise when he finds himself frequently unemployed because of his inability to keep a job. Sometimes a marriage starts with the husband being a student and having a limited income or none at all. In this case the wife may support him and be glad to do so. Occasionally she may offer her savings to keep him for this period of time, or she may even contribute to the raising of capital for a business venture. Many of these sacrifices on the part of wives lead to successful outcomes, but occasionally the husband leaves for another woman and the wife is left with a deep sense of bitterness, having given her all to him, only to be suddenly abandoned for somebody else. In these circumstances a wife's bitterness may lead to the most acrimonious divorce proceedings over financial arrangements.

Usually couples both work at the beginning of marriage and the wife often stops when she has a baby. Many women then withdraw from the labour market for a number of years whilst their children are young and return to work later on. It is during the time when wives are unemployed that they become particularly dependent on their husbands. Ceasing to work means not only financial dependence but the loss of the support that work gives. This support is a combination of friendship and affirmation. Through work men and women socialize, and thus broaden their human contacts, and also are reassured about their competence by seeing the results of their endeavours. This growth of confidence through achievement is of course also attained in and through childcare, and there is a need not to undervalue the significance of mothering.

But for some women the lack of human contact, the loss of reassurance from work, the personal and family economic deprivation and ultimately the diminution of status, combine to make staying at home intolerable and they return to employment as soon as possible. For a small number of women continuity of work is vital for their profession. When a woman with a young baby returns to employment, she needs the support of her husband, however much assistance she may get from help in the home. Such a woman needs to feel her husband supports her, is willing to make sacrifices on her behalf, help at home, be prepared to interrupt work suddenly and attend to the children if they are ill, be available during their holidays later on and generally be far more supportive. Most husbands are prepared to do this.

Some husbands however object all the way. They discourage the return to work and will only yield when they see clearly that their wife is being made ill or deeply unhappy by staying at home. They are unwilling to help or intervene on her behalf and expect life to run as if she did not have the combined responsibility of work and home. Whenever anything goes wrong, she is reminded that the difficulties are of her own choice.

(f) Leisure

One of the principal differences between the single state and marriage is the freedom to do what pleases one in the former and restriction in the latter. This restriction is linked with making oneself available to one's spouse for exclusive togetherness, socializing, visiting relatives and generally meeting the partner's needs.

Once again husbands often err by getting married and wanting the advantages of married life whilst attempting to retain their bachelor activities. They will continue to visit their friends at the pub, go to soccer matches, play cricket, rugby, soccer, hockey at the weekend, all at the expense of being with their wife.

Arguments may begin when the husband refuses to give up his leisure activities, insists that his wife gives up hers and comes with him, will not visit her relatives and is disinclined to have them at home, spends his spare time doing things that are of interest to him and finally brings work home — all of which limits his availability to his wife. Rarely, the wife may persist in visiting her home, sisters, brothers at his expense.

Clearly a balance between togetherness and separateness is the ideal, with togetherness distributed between socializing with others and being just with each other. Some couples find that they can only function together when they are in company with others. When they are alone, they cannot interact, indeed many simply argue or quarrel.

In conclusion, it can easily be seen that the social dimension plays a considerable part in the life of the couple at all times but is crucial during this phase when the relationship is being established. Conflicts in the social area frequently have emotional overtones, because the various aspects discussed impinge vitally on the couple and give a powerful taste of the quality of life. If their social experience is markedly disappointing, this colours widely their sense of well-being and influences adversely the continuation of the relationship.

2. The sexual dimension

Sexual intercourse is an encounter which has three meanings. It is responsible for a powerful instinctual pleasure often experienced in orgasm but not always so. There is an encounter, through the physical, between persons who affirm their love for each other and thirdly it is the means of starting new life. Thus its importance cannot be exaggerated.

In the early years, as indeed throughout marriage, two

factors are intimately linked with sex. First, in the presence of intact functioning, there is the quality of sexual life expressed in the preparation, actual experience and the aftermath of sexual intercourse. Secondly, in the presence of satisfactory quality, there is the issue of intact functioning in terms of adequate sexual drive and therefore frequency of intercourse, potency and ejaculation on the part of the man, ability to be penetrated and enjoy coitus without pain in the woman.

Sometimes in these early years women find that their husband spends no time preparing them for intercourse, has sex and then turns his back and goes to sleep. This treatment makes them feel that they are not persons but sexual objects, and this leads to marked resentment which will gradually increase with the passage of time.

When the quality of intercourse is good for both partners there remains the matter of function. In this phase the couple may discover that they cannot consummate their marriage. The husband may suffer from problems with impotence or premature ejaculation and the wife may be unable to enjoy intercourse, or to have an orgasm, or she may experience pain during coitus.

During these early years intercourse is likely to be frequent and meet the sexual needs of both partners, but even in this phase the husband may feel that he wants more sex than his wife.

Thus in these five years the foundations of discontent may be laid, for the husband in feeling sexually deprived and for the wife who feels she is treated as a sexual object rather than a person. The difficulties in function are understood much better nowadays and referral to a specialist unit is often helpful. Statistics suggest that in this phase some 12 — 18 per cent of marriages encounter sexual difficulties. A proportion of these improve with time and as the newer techniques of assistance become available this number will increase, but clearly a certain degree of dissatisfaction may remain and influence the marriage adversely at a later stage.

3. The emotional dimension

There is little doubt that the emotional dimension is crucial in contemporary marriage. As the main theme of this book suggests, marriages survive if the partners feel that they are loved, at least minimally, in terms of satisfaction and fulfilment in the five parameters I have indicated.

The emotional dimension is difficult to describe and every author has a different approach. Here, as in the rest of the book, I present what appears most commonly in the practice of counselling. At least three aspects of this dimension are heard repeatedly, namely the pattern of relating, the expression of feelings and the presence and resolution of conflict.

Pattern of relating

(a) *Freedom.* Some marriages, whether they are preceded by living together or not, break down suddenly and early in this phase. A close examination may reveal that the restriction of personal freedom coupled with the demands of the spouse prove beyond the ability of one or both partners. In this situation they feel trapped and are desperate to escape at the earliest opportunity.

(b) *Dominance.* Here the husband or wife, but frequently the former, takes charge of the relationship. He dominates the partner by insisting on having his way. He must be obeyed and not contradicted, and this means in practice that he creates an enormous fuss when his wishes are not met or an independent action is followed from the one he laid down. Following the insistence on having his way, he often disapproves of everything which does not conform to his notion of what his wife and later on his children should be, think and do. He needs to take the initiative and tolerates contradiction poorly.

Such dominance is sometimes associated with an inability to let his wife out of sight. He follows her as much as he can, closely questions her about her activities when she is out of sight and behaves in a jealous manner.

The dominant spouse often marries a submissive partner who at this stage of the marriage is happy to do as she is told, although as we shall see, this may not continue in the next phase. But there are wives or even husbands who rebel fairly quickly, and if they cannot persuade their spouse to change, they leave.

Dominance may be a feature of the personality, in the sense that a person may have supreme confidence in his outlook and feel that compromise is out of the question, but often this is not the case. The extremely dominant person is frequently covering up an enormous amount of anxiety and insecurity. In their childhood such people may have faced a dominating parent whom they imitate, but equally, they may have received a humiliating upbringing which they need to overcome by controlling others. Deep in the personality of the dominating person is a lack of confidence which cannot be faced and can only be negotiated by making sure that the spouse is never in a position to cause anxiety or insecurity. Such people behave in an all-or-nothing manner. They are going to be totally in charge and fear being totally annihilated if they yield an inch. When a wife or husband really insists on challenging the dominance of such a spouse, they are often surprised how the latter can collapse, like a pack of cards, for underneath the extreme dominance lies a frightened dependence. This is often discovered when a wife suddenly departs only to find her husband pleading, on his knees, crying and behaving in a desperate manner. It is often this desperation at being abandoned which lies behind the insistence of one spouse that their partner is constantly by their side. The childhood experiences of those who feel easily threatened with abandonment are full of insecurity and anxiety of personal loss.

(c) *Dependence*. The dominant person often marries someone who is emotionally dependent. The dependent person has frequently the opposite characteristics of the dominant person. He or she feels helpless, indecisive, needs constant reassurance, finds it difficult to take the initiative, gives up easily, is frightened and/or anxious and so cannot afford to displease, argue or contradict. At the heart of dependence is the feeling of incompleteness, inadequacy and a strong sense of needing another to make functioning possible. This dependence and immaturity are often linked. The dependent person lives in fear and often resents their state. Feeling unable to be angry they are constantly sniping in an indirect way by teasing, making nasty jokes, focusing on any weakness of the dominant person and being merciless if the latter falters in any way.

The dependent person has yet to outgrow their childish fears, need for guidance and support. They are often looking for authority to guide them. But gradually they outgrow their dependence or fear of aloneness and, as we shall see in the second phase, this can play havoc with the marital relationship.

Communicating affection

A couple will usually communicate affection through words, looks, touch or actions. Common complaints at this stage are that the spouse, often the husband, will not talk, nor will he show appreciation, praise or behave in a courteous manner. On the contrary he or she will be constantly critical, never pleased or satisfied with what has been done. Husbands call this nagging and wives often feel it as a rejection.

There is a particular problem when a husband or wife wants a lot of touching, such as holding, embracing and physical intimacy which is not necessary sexual and their partner finds this difficult. This conflict can be overcome with gradual expansion of contact.

Quarrelling

Every couple has a quarrel occasionally. Often a quarrel starts with disagreement about values, a decision on action or the way to do something, over what and how something is said or the feeling of being hurt. Most disagreements reach a compromise or an agreement to disagree. Apologies are offered and accepted, with forgiveness featuring frequently in reconciliation. At the heart of a successful quarrel lies the possibility of advancing mutual understanding and appreciation of the other's point of view, learning what hurts and avoiding it, making sure there is no victor and no sense of feeling defeated or humiliated.

But when quarrelling goes wrong the results are different. Here one spouse feels he must triumph, be right and the other made wrong or be reduced to guilt. Such a spouse can never be in the wrong and if proved to be so, never apologizes, never takes the initiative in reconciliation and ultimately withdraws into a sulk which may last from hours to weeks. Often such a husband or wife is an extremely sensitive person who, on close examination, is found to be totally unable to feel in the wrong or accept responsibility for wrongdoing. Childhood experiences of rejection, humiliation, criticism, coupled with an anxious make-up, make the sense of being at fault feel as if one is utterly bad, nasty and wicked, and this is accompanied by such pain of guilt and distress that admission of fault is hell. Such a sensitive person is often condemned as being intolerant, rigid, self-centred and other pejorative terms, not appreciating that for them an apology is the equivalent of personal annihilation. When this is recognized, progress can be made. If such a sensitive person, who has to make everyone responsible for his wrong-doing, marries someone who feels easily guilty and blameworthy there is a very unstable alliance which again may break up immediately or in the second stage.

Such alliances are technically called collusion, a term which designates a relationship in which the failure of maturation or the fantasy world of one partner matches, in the opposite direction, the equivalent immaturity and fantasy of the other. Thus the dominating spouse marries a dependent or submissive one, and the apparently insensitive partner (i.e. the one who cannot face his/her anxiety, fear, guilt, aggression) marries a sensitive partner who is ready to make the deficiencies of their partner their own fault and responsibility. Such collusive arrangements are basically unstable when one partner matures and refuses to continue to be a scapegoat for the other.

4. The intellectual dimension

Courtship usually ensures that a couple have, if not a similar, at least a close outlook on life and are likely to share similar educational, social and intellectual views. Politically they may often differ but this does not matter. Sometimes couples marry in a hurry or against their better judgement, only to find that months or weeks later they have nothing in common; this leads to an inevitable separation.

But the crucial aspect of the intellectual dimension is how

a couple communicate. The refusal of one spouse, often the husband, to discuss anything of depth and the tendency to concentrate on superficialities has already been mentioned. But when a couple discuss matters that are of importance to them, two problems may appear. The first is the rejection of the other's point of view without listening or paying attention to it, or the constant dismissal even after listening carefully. This attitude is rare. A far more common problem is where one spouse, usually the husband, relies on reason and the wife on feeling and/or intuition. Such different approaches can lead to marked clashes, with one branding the other as mistaken when in fact both can be correct. The wife feels in these circumstances that her husband is didactic, preaching to her the conclusions of the rational approach, whilst he may dismiss her in desperation with 'What can you expect from a woman?' Sometimes one partner is exhibiting the idealistic theory of how things should be, will be, can be, whilst the other is insisting on the practical implications. All these differences are legitimate, provided the spouse does not feel dismissed in his/her approach.

5. The spiritual dimension

A couple usually share the same faith or set of values, or else one tolerates the beliefs of the other even if they are not shared. When a spouse is attacked or humiliated for their beliefs, this is likely to lead to pain, distress and even departure. More often couples learn to adjust to their differences and to accommodate each other.

Children

The first phase of marriage ends with the advent of children. This is generally the result of a combined decision or at least the absence of resistance by the partner. Children transform the life of the couple, and it is important that the child is not experienced as an unwanted intrusion.

Pre-marital or early-in-marriage pregnancies can be experienced as an intrusion, and there is overwhelming evidence that these are connected with a high rate of marriage breakdown. At this stage husbands may abandon their wives or, rarely, wives may depart leaving their husband to cope with the baby.

The arrival of a baby is often associated with, at least initially, the giving up of work by the mother, an increase in fatigue, less time for the parents to be together, temporary reduction in sexual activity and for some women post-puerperal depression, irritability and loss of libido. The stresses on the marriage vary but in some instances are considerable and the marriage breaks up there and then. Often the difficulties leave a train of distress which is remembered long afterwards and forms one of the complaints in the second stage of marriage. Thus wives may complain that their husbands did not help them enough, insisted that life should continue unaltered, left them for business commitments when they were urgently needed, ignored them and the birth of the child by not visiting at the hospital or had an affair at this time. Husbands may complain that they lost their wife to the baby, that she changed or that their sexual life suffered permanently thereafter.

Conclusion

It can now be seen why this phase of marriage is so crucial. It establishes the basic relationship of the couple, and the high rate of break-up during this phase suggests that one or both partners did not feel that their minimum needs were being met. Some of these dissolutions are inevitable, because the couple are totally unsuited to each other. Appropriate help may preserve others.

Where a couple seek help, they will confront the counsellor with feelings of not experiencing sufficient love. The counsellor, having listened to the story, will assess the contributing factors, agree as far as possible with the couple what these are, and assist them in overcoming the crucial problems. The advantages of counselling in this phase are that good will, hope and determination are still present and these assets can be harnessed to overcome the difficulties. The disadvantages are the sense of futility of persevering when things go wrong so early, and feelings of marked insecurity that the partner cannot be trusted or that they are incapable of loving. Thus the difficulties in these early years can be seen as expected obstacles to be negotiated or intolerable burdens to be abandoned at once. If spouses still love and feel loved, effort is made, but when this is lost the marriage is doomed.

A simple and helpful rule of thumb in counselling at this and every stage is to find out at some point during the interview whether the spouses want to remain together. If both wish to do so, effective counselling should ensure this result. When one or both are really determined not to do so, the best counselling in the world is not likely to bring about a reconciliation. The greatest and commonest challenge as to the outcome is the presence of hesitant uncertainty in one or both partners. Here the quality of the counselling can make all the difference.

Further reading

B. Thornes and J. Collard, *Who Divorces?* Routledge and Kegan Paul, 1979 (ch. 6).

Sexual therapy:

F. Belliveau and L. Richter, *Understanding Human Sexual Inadequacy.* Coronet Books, 1971.
A. Comfort, *The Joy of Sex.* Simon and Schuster, New York, 1972.
H. Kaplan, *The New Sex Therapy.* Penguin, 1974.

Emotional dimension:

G. R. Bach and P. Wyden, *The Intimate Enemy: How to Fight Fair in Love and Marriage.* Souvenir Press, 1969.
C. J. Sager, *Marriage Contracts and Couple Therapy.* Brunner Mazel, New York, 1976.

Children:

C. F. Clulow, *To Have and to Hold.* Aberdeen University Press, 1982.
B. Thornes and J. Collard, *Who Divorces?* (ch. 7).

TEN

Second Phase: The Middle Years

This phase spans the two decades from thirty to fifty and is characterized by two features, developing awareness and, far more important, change.

Developing awareness

The problems mentioned in the first phase are either directly observed by the couple or are interpretations made by the counsellor. Where the couple reach the conclusions, it is pertinent to ask how they arrived at their formulation. How do partners appreciate that their relationship is problematic? It has already been mentioned that women realize earlier than men that a difficulty exists, are anxious to do something about it more frequently than their husbands and are more willing to talk to a counsellor. But how do women apprehend the difficulties? First they experience a contrast between what they expect or have been brought up to believe is appropriate and actuality. Secondly they may feel intuitively uncomfortable. Thirdly they may sense that what is happening is beyond the level of adaptation they should be expected to accept. Fourthly, they compare and contrast their life with that of their friends, neighbours and what they read and see on television.

So gradually they begin to realize that an aspect of their life is not only difficult but, if it persists, is becoming a problem. It is in the early years of this second phase that spouses often begin to define their difficulties as problems and are anxious to seek help when they feel that the presence of these problems is intolerable or threatens the marriage.

Thus couples who come for help during this phase may often complain about matters which belong exclusively to the first phase. There is an intimate continuity between the first and second phase but the exact timing of recognizing a problem, even if it has existed for a number of years, may be due to the fact that a spouse experiences additional distress. A physical illness, a catastrophe in the family, the death of a parent or close relative, a depressive illness, may all lower the patience and tolerance of a spouse, and the combination of long standing problems, aggravated by a fresh adversity, precipitates a crisis, the decision to seek help or sometimes to leave abruptly.

Change

What is specific however about the second phase is the impact of change. Partners may alter during these years in one or more of the five dimensions and this alteration is responsible for another major contribution to marital conflict. Change will be considered in all the five dimensions.

Social
One feature of social change is the advent of success at work with its financial and social advantages. This success often comes to the husband but may also apply to the wife. In the latter case the husband may feel threatened, become envious and may even attempt to undermine the wife's success. When the husband becomes successful he may express it in a new house, material plenitude, manifestations of wealth, a new set of social acquaintances, further ambition, sometimes in the political field, and a new outlook of prominence and inflated ego. The wife may welcome and adapt to all this, or she may be left well behind, unable to cope, or she may rebel against values which clash with her outlook on life. Often success means more commitments for the husband and less time for the family. The wife finds herself having less of her husband, being expected to entertain and go out with his new circle of friends and sometimes to give up her own long-standing friendships. In these circumstances she may feel that she is gradually losing her husband to a world whose priorities she does not trust. If she needs a good deal of his time and personal attention, the loss becomes seriously threatening, and in the midst of plenty she becomes increasingly depressed, a response which baffles her husband.

In fact, men who are successful providers are often confused by the disappointment of their wives, who would like some time with them and better communication, even at the expense of a lower standard of living.

Upward social mobility contrasts with a downward movement which is of course a more common cause of problems. Persistent illness, unemployment, alcoholism and gambling are the commonest reasons for social loss of status. Either partner may be affected, but unemployment and alcoholism are more often male problems. Spouses do not often abandon their partner in adversity except when their psychological make-up cannot tolerate the deprivation and lack of support. The presence of such adversity leads to frequent arguments, a rise of irritability, and a spouse may depart because they cannot tolerate the stress in their life. Sometimes spouses will leave home but remain friends with their partner, to whom they will return if the problem, often alcohol, is given up.

So far reference has been made to social mobility, but during this phase spouses may change the direction of their life by giving up their work and undertaking something new. Business is changed for a religious or social work career, different employment is taken up, town is given up for the country, work is chosen abroad, retirement from the armed forces—these are all common examples. The spouse may or may not adapt to such changes. Sometimes the husband comes from a position of authority or security, such as the armed forces, and finds himself lost in civilian life for which he is totally unsuited, particularly missing the supportive structure of an authoritarian institution. In all these situations marriages may suffer as a change in job reveals character weaknesses which were hidden in a hierachical and supportive environment.

Finally continuous unemployment can have devastating effects on men who lose their sense of dignity and self-esteem, becoming depressed and anxious, withdrawing from their wives and children into a world of their own where they cannot be reached.

Sexual
The common sexual problems were mentioned in the first

phase. In this phase any initial poverty in the sexual relationship will be increasingly recognized and may be found unacceptable. In particular, infrequent sex will make its adverse impact and couples may seek help, having had no sex for months or even years. Functional problems, such as impotence and premature ejaculation, become more frequent in the forties, and depressive illness, which affects both sexes but women more often, may impair libido.

The specific sexual problems in this phase are twofold. First there may be a persistent post-puerperal loss of sexual desire in the wife. At the extreme end of this state such a woman has no sexual feelings and cannot tolerate being touched erotically, although she wants physical affection. This condition needs urgent expert attention because it may destroy the marriage. Secondly, the sexual relationship may deteriorate because of difficulties in the other dimensions. In these situations direct sexual help is of no avail until the relationship improves.

Finally extra-marital affairs, which will be considered in chapter 13, occur with increasing frequency during these two decades. The specific sexual impact of an affair on a woman, whatever its personal significance, is the fact that she may discover that, for the first time, she enjoys intercourse and even has an orgasm. Up to now, she was aware of sexual disappointment, but had no criterion by which to judge the husband's performance or her response. Now she knows better and henceforth her husband will be judged by new standards. At a time of increased permissiveness some women have sexual experience with a number of men before they marry and know what they are capable of. But there are still many wives who confine intercourse to their husband, so they have no means of assessing the quality of their sexual life.

The combination of a woman with an initial limited interest in sex and a husband with low libidinal drive may present no problems in the first phase but do so during this one when the drive of the wife improves and she wants more sex. A husband may be placed under considerable pressure to offer more sex as his wife learns how to relax and enjoy intercourse. Often he cannot do much to improve his sexual performance, and this combination presents a special problem in this phase. It is one which may be insoluble except when the wife accepts, as a substitute, more physical affection and the husband learns to offer this in terms of cuddling, embracing and physical closeness.

Emotional

This is one area which sees marked and vital changes during this period.

(a) *Unconscious-conscious.* This is the phase when behaviour, which has been influenced by unconscious factors, may reach the surface of consciousness. This can be brought about most clearly by psychological help, but this is rare. Insight may be achieved in the way already described, by reflecting consciously on childhood, through dreams which are really revelations, and of course most important of all by commentaries on one's behaviour from the spouse and trusted friends. Gradually awareness deepens and the relationship is seen in a new light which may disclose the depths of discontent, or the distress may be hidden by becoming depressed.

(b) *Dependence-Independence.* The typical dependent spouse, often the wife, has already been described. The main features which make her comply with a dominating partner are fear, anxiety, lack of confidence and self-esteem. As a result of personal growth, through having children, work, encouragement from friends and her social network, what she reads and sees on television and other more obscure maturing processes, such a wife begins to find herself.

This self-discovery is a complex process. She starts to feel that she possesses herself, in other words is in charge of her own life which no longer belongs to her parents or parent substitute, namely her husband. A wife summed this up well when she said: 'All my life I have done what others want me to do. First it was my parents and then my husband. Now I want to do what I want.' Secondly, she feels she has a right to her own choices and decisions. She is no longer prepared to subordinate her inclinations to those of her husband, a transformation which may lead to large-scale rebellion. Thirdly, she wants to take the initiative, experiment, find out for herself what life is about, which means independent action. If her husband needs constant reassuring closeness or feels threatend that her independence will mean alienation and loss of her to somebody else, his anxiety rises and there are further bitter arguments.

As a result of these changes a wife begins to take command of her life. She may want to learn how to drive a car, seek her own friends, do things for herself, go to work, take the initiative with holidays or even demand separate ones, argue with her husband and refuse to behave in the way she has done for several years. This growth is something which happens to a lesser extent in all marriages presenting both spouses with the need for mutual adaptation. When the growth is unilateral, the dominating husband cannot believe what he is witnessing. He protests and tries to block the change. There are many skirmishes, gathering momentum and becoming fierce battles. The wife becomes adamant, and when the husband refuses to modify his attitude, the marriage is in disarray and may break down.

Quarrels increase in frequency and severity, and physical violence may occur. The husband cannot understand what is happening and the change of his wife's behaviour simply raises his anxiety to panic proportions. Tension is very high, and the ensuing anger of the wife makes her withdraw sexually, rendering an already difficult situation almost impossible. At this point, which may be reached only after years, the wife simply walks out and never returns. She makes up her mind to depart and may go to another relationship or live alone. Sometimes she wants to go but is afraid actually to leave, in which case she may become depressed or even attempt suicide as she feels trapped in an impossible situation.

(c) *Dominance.* The commonest patterns of break-down result from the growth of independence. But occasionally the dominant person tires of supporting their dependent partner and decides to go. They may form a new relationship in which they feel supported for the first time or simply decide to live alone.

(d) *Self-esteem and lovability.* In the process of maturation,

women and men, who started the marriage with a poor image
of themselves, considerable feelings of inadequacy, a sense of
badness and a high degree of guilt, gradually find that their
rejection of themselves is not justified. Poor self-esteem is
often the result of a childhood in which parents criticized and
rejected them, or, failing to affirm their offspring, inculcated
in them a sense of badness and guilt, so that they grew up
without the sense of feeling lovable. Sometimes poor self-
esteem is the result of the presence of marked anxiety. Such a
self-rejecting person, who feels unlovable, may marry,
obviously for unconscious reasons, a partner who is also
critical, shows little love and generates guilt. The spouse with
poor self-esteem accepts all this initially as normal, but
gradually they find that they are not so bad, become more
aware of their need for love and realize that their partner
makes them feel guilty and bad because he or she cannot
accept their own shortcomings and projects them onto their
spouse. There is a gradual awareness that, if they want more
love, they are not selfish and demanding, as they had been
told first by their parents and then by their husband. In brief,
they realize for the first time that they are lovable, a feeling
which was either denied to them from childhood onwards or
has not been one they have been able to register up to now.

(e) *Identity.* As a result of all this new awareness, spouses
who develop late begin to acquire a new identity for
themselves. They develop a new image which feels good,
lovable and worthy of care, appreciation and attention, and
they no longer feel guilty about their requirements. The
significance of this discovery can be easily realized. It feels
like being born again. Life develops a meaning hitherto
undreamed of, and nothing in the world is going to stop the
development of a new style of living.

It takes a great deal of maturity and commitment to the
marriage not to abandon it at once and seek a new relationship
which will do justice to the newly discovered self. Often the
husband is seen as the real enemy. His dominance produces
hate, and it is the counsellor who has to remind the wife that
it was she who chose him at a time when her personality
needed his authoritarian approach. The realization that all
the years of feeling guilty and bad were unnecessary and that

these feelings were reinforced by the husband, who made her a scapegoat because of his own immaturity, may produce deep rage. It is the counsellor once again who has to remind her of her unconscious invitation to be treated as bad and made to feel guilty.

The need to gain independence, experience love and escape from any further sense of guilt may make such a wife insist that she leaves her husband and the breakdown rate of these marriages is high. Good counselling, which recognizes the complexity of the situation and clarifies it, may save some of them, but sometimes the wife still leaves on the grounds that the man she married is no longer relevant to her life, which now requires a totally new form of complementarity. Even more starkly, the thought of remaining with her husband mobilizes so many unpleasant memories that she simply wants to close this chapter in her life and start afresh.

It can be seen why emotional change is so important and the heavy contribution it makes to marital breakdown. An essential part of preventing marital breakdown is to help couples who are in this predicament begin to seek help at a much earlier stage, before bitterness spoils the relationship. This is of course much easier said than done, but it is possible.

Intellectual

Part of the growth of confidence in a husband or wife, but particularly the latter, is to discover that neither her approach to her life nor her way of arguing is silly. There is an increasing trust in one's own judgement, which leads to challenging the spouse with an enhanced tenacity. If the spouse persists in dismissing their partner, he or she may get fed up and seek recognition elsewhere.

Spiritual

A couple may start with a common faith which is practised, and often one gives it up. This causes pain and may aggravate other problems but is rarely a cause, itself, for divorce.

But the values of couples change. Husbands may look with horror at their emancipating wives, accusing them of rampant feminism. Perhaps the most common conflict in values is the situation where one spouse seeks material advantages and the other wants simplicity, time for each other and the children. The approach to their children may also lead to a lot of conflict. Disagreements may ensue about the children's education or about moral values and behaviour. Parents may differ on matters of discipline, sexual mores, expressions of freedom and money allowances. When one parent takes an attitude which is not backed by the other, he or she may feel betrayed and unsupported. Once again, differences over children do not by themselves lead to divorce, but they can aggravate a precarious marital situation.

Conclusion

This is the phase of marriage when divorce most frequently occurs, even though many of the reasons emanate from the first phase. The specific contribution of this period is widespread change, which has to be recognized by the counsellor and the marked bitterness and vehemence of the emancipating spouse appreciated. But it is also necessary to recognize that such changes cause marked anxiety to the other spouse, who often has little idea of what is happening and is petrified of losing their partner.

Further reading

J. Coleman, *The Nature of Adolescence.* Methuen, 1980.

M. Lauffer, *Adolescent Behaviour and Breakdown.* Penguin, 1975.

B. Musgrave and Z. Merrall (ed.), *Change and Choice, Women and Middle Age.* Peter Owen, 1980.

G. O'Collins, *The Second Journey; Spiritual Awareness and the Mid-life Crisis.* Villa Books, Dublin, 1979.

L. Pincus (ed.), *Marriage; Studies in Emotional Growth and Conflict.* Methuen, 1960.

K. Soddy and M. Kitson, *Men in Middle Life.* Tavistock Publications, 1967.

ELEVEN

Third Phase: The Later Years

The third phase has been designated as lasting from the age of fifty to the death of one spouse. It is a period during which the children leave home or marry, grandchildren arrive and the couple return to a one-to-one relationship. Finally one has to face the illness and death of their spouse. Usually it is a period of relative tranquility and fulfilment and may last twenty years or more — the widespread length of this phase being relatively new in the West. Nevertheless marriages do break down during this period.

Marriages being brought to counsellors at this stage may show any of the features of the first stage or aspects of change and maturation which have been delayed. The features which mark new discord at this point are not clearly understood and often overlap with events in the late stages of the second phase.

Social

The position of male employment is rapidly deteriorating in the West, and unemployment is the most likely issue affecting this phase. When the husband is ready to cease working no problem exists, but if he is unprepared or unwilling to stop, the stress in his life is unloaded on his wife who may not be able to cope with it. Sometimes the problem is not unemployment but thwarted ambition. A man may feel strongly that he should be promoted, and if this does not happen he becomes frustrated, morose and even withdrawn, all of which taxes his wife.

Finally a man may be promoted and find that his new job is beyond his capabilities, which makes him anxious or even depressed, and his wife has to cope with this pressure. In all these situations the wife may have to bear the burdens of her husband. Usually this is a nuisance but is no threat to the marriage except where other adverse factors exist.

Another factor is the ageing of the spouses' parents. This may make heavy demands on the marriage which cannot easily sustain such stress. If a parent dies, the other may need to reside with the couple, and if this is opposed by either partner there is further strain, particularly when it is interpreted as a personal rejection.

At about the same time the children are leaving home and getting married. One spouse may find the departure of the children a severe loss and need the support of their partner to negotiate it. If he/she remains unavailable this can cause much distress.

Sexual

During the early part of this phase the wife has her menopause. Normally this is a biological event with no adverse consequences on her sexual life, but when the latter has been poor for some time the menopause can be used as an excuse for discontinuing further sex. Hysterectomy may also be used in this way. However women do not usually lose their sexual drive during this phase. Indeed, freed from the anxieties of procreation, some of them experience a new sense of sexual well-being and are very much sexually alive. This places a responsibility on husbands, who have also been shown to have a sexual capacity that survives well during these years. But there is evidence that problems, in the form of impotence, do afflict a small number of men during this period and, if the marriage relies heavily on sexual satisfaction, the loss of intercourse can be most stressful. These couples should be referred for expert help because in some instances recovery of function can take place.

When sex is no longer possible, physical affection is an important way of remaining close, and it is the loss of sex combined with the inability to show affection physically, that is a source of stress.

Emotional

Most of the emotional problems of this phase have a long history behind them and can be traced to earlier periods.

However the commonest reason for marital breakdown during this period is the pattern whereby a couple whose children have left home suddenly discover that they have nothing in common with each other. Despite the fact that they have lived together for many years, slept together, made love and eaten from the common table, no deep relationship was established. Without realizing it, spouses lived through the children and/or their respective work. When the children go, they see in each other a social friend and an emotional stranger. They may agree to stay together but sleep in separate bedrooms, go on their holidays alone and follow their own interests, but equally they may decide to split up. When one partner wants to go and the other to remain then separation can be extremely painful for the one who remains behind.

As already referred to in the second phase, a supportive spouse may get tired of their increasing task of protection and leave.

Intellectual and spiritual

This is a phase of life when intellectual powers change gradually into wisdom and often there is a flowering of faith or spiritual values. Couples tend to have contributed to this mutual growth and usually enjoy and appreciate each other. When there has been little contact with each other at a deep personal level, there is a marked alienation in these areas which dictates mutual silence over disagreements.

Conclusion

The most helpful contribution that a marriage counsellor can make to a couple in this stage of marriage is to facilitate the recovery of at least a minimum of mutual satisfaction so the decades spent together do not appear wasted, but, when no real mutual relationship ever existed, a late separation may be the only realistic solution despite all the pain it causes.

Further reading

I. Deutscher, 'The Quality of Post-Parental Life; definitions of the situation'. *(Journal of Marriage and the Family,* 26, 52, 1964).

L. Pincus, *Death and the Family.* Faber, 1976.

C. M. Parkes, *Bereavement.* Penguin, 1975.

PART THREE

TWELVE

Indecision

Marriage counselling is needed in two situations which involve indecision. The first concerns the uncertainty of marrying. The second and more common, involves the difficult decision of leaving a marriage.

The decision to marry

In the course of marriage counselling one repeatedly hears accounts of marital consent being given reluctantly, against one's better judgement and in the presence of emotional coercion. There is little doubt that some of these feelings are later interpolations and these doubts did not exist initially. Nevertheless the persistence and often clear authenticity of these reflections suggests that many are accurate.

Here are some recurrent examples. The presence of a pregnancy used to be a common reason and it may still be one. Sometimes marriages take place immediately after a broken engagement or at the termination of a particularly precious relationship without due consideration and in haste. Some spouses claim that they did not wish to marry their partner, who put a lot of pressure on them, threatened to take his/her life and even attempted suicide. Many admit that they married without being in love but hoping that this would grow in the course of time. No doubt a number of marriages starting under such circumstances overcome the initial lack of enthusiasm and work out successfully. Commonsense suggests however that it is from the ranks of these doubtful commitments that a good deal of breakdown emerges, and it is worth examining the factors mentioned in some detail.

Undoubtedly marriages forced by pregnancy, in the absence of a loving relationship, are vulnerable, and the statistics of divorce give ample evidence for this. No marriage should be forced on reluctant parents. The modern solution of the termination of pregnancy is no solution either, and a good deal of thought and care needs to go to save both the life of the baby and the integrity of the parents if no marriage is undertaken.

Time should always intervene between the termination of one intimate relationship and the conclusion of the next relationship in marriage. The loss of a special relationship leads to feelings of depression, resentment, loneliness, all of which may hasten a marriage which is unlikely to succeed.

There are men and women who feel desperately the need to marry and put pressure on reluctant partners, even sometimes by threats of suicide. Such threats should be resisted, and when hesitation exists the decision to marry should be postponed. Similarly a spouse may feel friendly towards their lover but not be in love with them. A distinction must be made between friendship and being in love and the former is not a sound basis for matrimony.

These doubts are so important that every one entertaining them should have a chance to discuss them, and inquiry about the degree of certainty and commitment to the spouse should form an essential part of the marriage preparation. *The pastor should see the couple separately and feel sure that serious doubt does not exist.*

Research has shown that there are some people whose doubts reach panic proportions and they suffer an acute anxiety or depressive state as the date of the marriage approaches. Postponing the date or even the decision to marry brings relief but the disturbance returns when a new date is arranged and it begins to get close. Such men and women need to be referred for psychological help.

But how is any counsellor to distinguish between normal anxieties about a pending marriage and serious doubts which should be heeded? There are no certain answers but some guidelines do exist. The important distinction is between, on the one hand, experiencing discomfort or even anxiety about the pending marriage but having no doubts about the future spouse and, on the other, having serious reservations about the actual partner. In the latter case, delay and further careful examination of one's feeling should take place.

Given that no marriage is likely to be contemplated in the absence of some affection, the real questions concern sexual attraction and social compatibility. It is worth repeating the statement that friendship is not the same as marriage, and both sex and a common social life are crucial for the viability of a relationship. On the other hand sexual attraction alone without other affinities is unlikely to survive.

The decision to leave

Many counsellors, pastors and indeed almost everyone is sooner or later asked by a spouse whether they should stay or not in an unhappy marriage. The first rule in this situation, as in the matter of marriage itself, is never to reply in an affirmative or negative manner. This decision belongs to the individual and no one should decide for them. Furthermore there are certain people such as ministers of religion and those with a committed belief against divorce who are expected to counsel continuation of the marriage. Their views in principle are well known and simple reiteration of the obvious is not helpful. What is constructive is to take a person through the five dimensions of marriage and assess what elements are still remotely viable.

Clearly when a spouse examines the five areas and finds that there is nothing left which they share with their spouse, then this clarifies the situation. Whatever else may exist, it is certainly not marriage. Often this is the reality of the situation, as the spouse suspected but feared to acknowledge. A discussion magnifies the absence of any real relationship and allows the decision to be made with some degree of certainty.

But what happens when there is still some life in one or more dimension? Clearly what matters is the relationship between what is left and the needs of the individual. The reason why any married person wants to leave is that some basic need is not being met. It is the counsellor's task to help the person assess as clearly as possible what their basic needs are, what their partner can offer and whether compensation (e.g. affection replacing sex, social affinity replacing affection, or sexual compatibility replacing social, affectional or spiritual needs) can work. For most couples affection and sex are the primary needs but all sorts of combinations are potentially viable.

Clearly the less fulfilment a marriage offers, the greater is the need to accept some pain and sacrifice, if the marriage is to continue. The ability to pay such a price is a reflection of the character of the individual, their faith or value system.

Nowadays there is an increasing tension between commitment to a relationship, however empty, and personal fulfilment. The counsellor, even a minister of religion, cannot live any one else's life. What he can do is to clarify the situation, support any honest and conscientious decision, inject hope and encouragement whatever the decision is and to avoid inculcating guilt if the marriage is abandoned.

What happens when a Christian minister of religion is involved as a counsellor? His commitment to marital indissolubility is not likely to be in doubt, and he will be expected to support every effort to sustain the marriage. Equally, as a representative of Christ, he is bound to be understanding, merciful and forgiving. If the decision is to leave the marriage, his task is to support the couple in their distress, ensure that the parting leaves as little enmity as possible and encourage the continuation of the practice of faith.

Sometimes the decision to leave becomes complicated further by the continuing uncertainty whether to persist with the departure. A man or a woman may leave and be overwhelmed by guilt feelings which pressurises them to return. Spouses may leave and take up residence with another man or woman for days or weeks and then come back home. This shuttlecock situation can continue for some time and leaves everyone exhausted. In these circumstances a marriage counsellor is often consulted.

Counselling takes the same form as before. The guilt feelings are examined and they usually consist of a combination of a sense of loss, the pain of losing familiar surroundings, the distress caused to the spouse, to the new partner and a marked doubt with whom one wants to live. These tensions can be overwhelming and place people in intolerable states of mind. Given this pain, the counsellor helps by examining with the individual the five parameters of marriage and what is available in the respective relationships. Once again it may be found that the existing marriage has no viable dimensions and the distress cannot be relieved by returning home. When there is viability in both relationships, the person has to be helped to find what is essential for her/him and what can be tolerated, particularly if adjustments are to be made in the marriage. Once again the same principles of character—values, faith, sacrifice and commitment—play a vital part.

Sometimes, despite an objective awareness of what should be done, a spouse keeps returning home only to depart after a short period. These returns cause havoc as they raise hope in the abandoned spouse and children only to dash them again. If there is really no hope of reconciliation, the forgiving spouse who accepts the partner back has to be helped to face the hopelessness of the situation and strengthened against further toleration of the departed partner.

There are however spouses who are determined never to give up their side of the commitment and remain permanently open to a return of their spouse, or, if no such possibility exists, to live their life with heroic determination of being faithful to their vows. Such attitudes are not held in high esteem at present, but whenever they are to be found they deserve admiration, encouragement and support.

Children

One of the most powerful reasons for not terminating a marriage is the presence of children, and the pain involved of leaving them behind can be intense. Precious as children are, they are not able to meet all the needs of adults and a counsellor, who is discussing with a client the decision to stay or go, must examine, as before, what is left of a relationship. Clearly when children are present and play a determining factor, spouses decide to stay even when there is very little in the relationship. In fact many marriages stay together for the sake of the children and, however poor the relationship is, neither parent contemplates separation. The separation may occur when the children grow up. When no children exist there is greater freedom to separate and an association between divorce and the absence of children exists.

Those who contemplate separation often ask what this will do to the children, and the advocates of divorce have maintained for a long time that children benefit from it when the parents cannot live together in harmony. These questions are easier to ask than to answer. Such research as exists suggests that children want their parents to stay together much more than is generally appreciated, and those who favour divorce for the sake of the children are not on strong ground here.

The impact of marital breakdown on children is a topic which requires a whole book on its own. The consequences depend on the sex of the child, its age, personality, the quality of parenting with the remaining parent, the degree and quality of contact with the departed one and the presence of a remarriage. There is no doubt that most children suffer immediate distress when a parent leaves, and this may last up to two years. The long-term impact is variable and sometimes will not be known until many decades later, but the ranks of people with personality disorders, neurotics, alcoholics, delinquents and those with psychiatric illness have an above average incidence of divorce in their families of origin. The association is undoubtedly complex and no one can indict divorce directly for any particular adverse consequence, but nor can its significance in childhood be dismissed.

Thus when parents ask about the possible damage to their children, the answer is that there will certainly be some immediate distress, which in some instances will be severe. The long-term impact is uncertain but all the available adverse evidence cannot be dismissed with impunity.

But what are the consequences if parents stay together for the sake of the children? There is evidence that, if the parents are constantly quarrelling, show violence and consequently the atmosphere in the home is tense, children suffer and boys in particular can develop aggressive, antisocial behaviour. Equally if the parents totally withdraw from each other, sleep in separate bedrooms and are living in bitterness and anger, the children do not see a model of love. Thus if parents are to stay together there is need for a minimum of courtesy and friendliness even if they are no longer loving each other. In the presence of such a civil atmosphere and when the parents can individually show love to their children, then the latter are certainly likely to benefit.

Overt hostility and enmity and the presence of constant

tension are damaging to the children, who may copy these patterns in their own life later on.

Further reading

D. L. Davies, 'Psychiatric Illness in those engaged to be married', *(British Journal of Social and Preventive Medicine,* 10, 123, 1956).

J. F. McDermott, 'Divorce and its Psychiatric Sequelae in Children', *(Archives of General Psychiatry,* 23, 421, 1970).

J. S. Wallerstein and J. B. Kelly, *Surviving the Breakdown.* Grant McIntyre, 1980.

THIRTEEN

Infidelity

Of all the behaviour that can be construed as an attack on marriage, infidelity is the one recognized by almost everyone as the most serious. The combination of a breach of commitment against exclusiveness and the violation of sexual faithfulness creates a sense of rejection and mistrust. Infidelity may be emotional, sexual or a combination of both. Whatever form it takes, but especially when extramarital intercourse is involved, it can arouse hurt, anxiety and a sense of betrayal. Statistics for extra-marital sexual activity are hard to establish, but even so, it is suggested that by the age of 40, some 25 per cent of wives and 50 per cent of men have participated in it. These figures given by Kinsey are probably on the low side, so that currently many marriages have to face this event.

Infidelity raises many issues. Perhaps the most crucial distinction is whether extra-marital sex is a casual event or an expression of a deeper personal involvement. It can be argued that only a debased sense of sex can ever make it a casual event. Nevertheless reality embraces a wide range of sexual activity. The real threat to a marriage arises from the desire to convert an affair into a permanent relationship.

What should the attitude of a spouse be in the presence of the adultery of their partner? The Christian ethic requires forgiveness, and indeed a great deal of adultery is forgiven although perhaps never forgotten. But in my view to forgive is not enough. An essential part of forgiveness is to go beyond it and understand the reasons for the behaviour. Sometimes the spouse who has committed adultery feels guilty, is forgiven and yet in the depths of their being knows that their partner drove them into it. If their partner cannot see the part they have played, little is resolved. Furthermore if the aggrieved spouse does not see their own contribution, a sense of righteousness enters their life with which they try to exercise moral control over their erring partner, who is never allowed to forget their misdeed.

Forgiveness without understanding is a very incomplete process and the role of the counsellor is to assist the process of clarification. With this object in mind, infidelity will be examined in the three stages of marriage.

The first phase

Extra-marital intercourse in these early years is particularly hurtful. It apparently contradicts the whole sense of commitment to the newly established relationship. What are the reasons?

First of all there are men and women who give advance notice of this behaviour by their sexual conduct during courtship. If a person shows distinct signs of promiscuous behaviour during courtship, this may well continue after marriage and indeed should not surprise anyone. The need to have frequent and varied sex has been accounted for by the presence of marked extrovert features in the personality. Such a person needs a high level of sexual activity and is not particularly concerned with whom this is realized. Don Juan is the representative of this group.

Next comes a personality which is much more disturbed, the man or woman who is variously called immature or psychopathic. Infidelity is part of a wide range of characteristics including poor work record, financial irresponsibility and aggressive behaviour. Such a person has yet to mature in terms of self-control, application, commitment and responsibility, and lives like a child in satisfying instincts without any further social or moral development.

Infidelity may take place when a spouse is away from home. The need for sex on these occasions may arise out of loneliness, boredom or a marked anxiety of feeling alone and insecure. Being away from home may also create a feeling of a return to the single state with all the independence and lack of responsibility that this means.

Sometimes men find any interruption of sexual intercourse during pregnancy or the period afterwards intolerable and may resort to casual affairs or even visit prostitutes. Adultery during this period is particularly hurtful to the wife.

Finally intercourse may take place with an ex-boy- or girl-friend when the marital relationship is going through a difficult period and the spouse wants comfort or solace. In particular during these early years, when both spouses are working, either may feel emotionally very deprived and, having failed to communicate this to their partner, they fall back on a familiar figure. When the encounter with the previous lover is discovered it constitutes a double threat, in the sense that the spouse is worried both about the marriage and also whether their partner is entertaining doubts and wants to live with the other person.

The second phase

Many of the reasons for adultery in the first phase also apply in the second. The specific features of the second phase arise from the deterioration of the relationship, emotionally or sexually.

As already shown, either spouse, but often the wife, may find during these years that she does not feel fulfilled in her relationship. She may be deprived sexually, if her sexual life is non-existent or markedly poor. She may be angry with a husband who is not appreciative of her newly developed personality. She often feels markedly short of attention and affection. In all these circumstances she is unconsciously looking for alternative experiences, even though not directly seeking an affair. Women in these situations suddenly find themselves having affairs at work, with the husband of a friend, or with a neighbour. They are startled when they discover what is happening. They often say, 'It is the last thing in the world I expected to happen to me.' However a close examination of the marital relationship will show profound gaps in satisfaction.

Husbands may also find their marriage unsatisfactory as sexual activity deteriorates following the birth of children, attention from their wives dwindles as they become busy with children and work, or as they alter in themselves and want to be treated differently. The opportunities for adultery have increased for both sexes in our society but they are always easier for men who have contacts at work or abroad.

In this phase infidelity is likely to be more than a passing experience and is often symptomatic of a serious deficiency in the relationship. When couples face infidelity in each other during these years the need for a deeper examination of the quality of the marriage is paramount.

During their forties men and women may experience doubts about their sexual performance and have an extra-marital relationship to reassure themselves about their capacities and attractiveness. Such affairs are a reminder of the vital importance of sexual intercourse not only for its pleasure content but also as a reassurance that the person behind the body is still desired. Sometimes an affair during these years may be the first intimation a woman has of being sexually successful. Constant disappointment at the hands of her husband and no previous experience may make her feel a sexual failure. The discovery of her competence may introduce a new dimension in the marriage as she now realizes the limitations of her husband, begins to challenge him about it and even urges him to seek help.

Thus affairs during these years may be an expression of persistent poor sexual activity which is no longer acceptable, a deterioration in the personal relationship and the unconscious seeking of comfort elsewhere, or a need for sexual reassurance. Every affair needs examination in the light of these possibilities, but in particular every effort should be made to appreciate the changing nature of the relationship which requires a different response from the spouse.

The third phase

All the reasons that apply in the first and second phase also apply in the third, but at this time it is especially an expression of a deteriorating personal relationship. Some men may experience early symptoms of impotence, sometimes associated with genito-urinary operations or venereal infections, and desperately need to be reassured. Occasionally men and women may mature late in life and seek sexual satisfaction for the first time during these years.

Infidelity and Sexual Values

All that has been said so far connects infidelity with some

disturbance in the personality, in the relationship or in sexual life itself, and indeed much extra-marital activity is linked in this way. But there are people who believe that sex is to be enjoyed as an end in itself without reference to love in personal relationships, or that sex has a social value and may be used as a form of payment for services rendered or in order to achieve a desirable goal.

Clearly if a person believes that sex should be pursued for its own specific pleasurable ends or linked with social purposes, then he or she is not likely to be over-scrupulous in how they behave. In fact part of the sexual revolution of the last twenty-five years is the development of so-called open marriages, where partners formulate rules whereby they can have extra-marital relationships without endangering the marriage. Such relationships are still a minute minority and no careful studies have been done over a period of time to assess their survival rate.

The problem exists when one spouse believes in sexual freedom and the other does not or is a reluctant partner. In the past it was the man's prerogative to enjoy this liberty and the duty of women to tolerate the consequences. Nowadays the remnants of this inequality can still be seen, but women are prepared to accept less and less of such behaviour. Sometimes they are prepared to accept it but also choose to behave in a similar manner. The fact remains that when one spouse believes or needs fidelity in their life and their partner flouts their wishes, then the result is likely to be painful conflict, which in the end may lead to marital breakdown.

Another variation to the complex problem of values may be seen in the marriage where the faithful partner adopts a high moral tone, is particularly critical of their spouse's infidelity and is the one who is not interested in sex, which they find unattractive or even disgusting. Such people are not capable of seeing that their fidelity is not an expression of discipline and effort but an inevitable association with poor sexual drive or lack of interest. Some people have an exaggerated sense of offence over adultery because they themselves are incapable of offending in this way. An equal hypocrisy is to be found in the person who has behaved irresponsibly in their youth and then later in life adopts a high moral tone.

Revelation

The marriage counsellor is often asked whether someone who has committed adultery should tell their partner. Once again direct advice should be avoided. The matter needs examination to discover what will be achieved by the revelation. If this is directed towards the improvement of the relationship then it has a justification. If it is meant to achieve an assuagement of guilt feelings or is prompted by childish inclinations which compel the admission of wrong-doing as a simple act of owning up, then clearly nothing will be gained except the infliction of pain on the partner. This pain is only justified when it can lead to a further positive development of the relationship.

Sometimes the marriage counsellor is told of infidelity which has not been revealed to the partner and is then asked to keep it confidential. All information given to a counsellor is confidential and must not be divulged even to the partner without prior permission. So confidences have to be respected. Sometimes however a counsellor is let into a secret which is far from being over. In other words he is being asked not only to receive the confidence but to help a marriage in which he is invited to be privy to an affair which is resolutely maintained. These are tricky matters, and each situation has to be treated on its own merits. Confidence must not be broken, but the counsellor may come to realize that he is being used to maintain both an affair and a marriage without the person involved having the slightest intention of making a decision; indeed they may be using the counselling situation as an excuse to continue both relationships. Whenever the counsellor recognizes that he is being used as part of a plan which threatens the honesty and integrity of both partners, he must avoid collaboration.

Further reading

L. Gross (ed.), *Sexual Issues in Marriage.* Spectrum Publications, New York, 1975.

FOURTEEN

Jealousy

The subject of jealousy is intimately related to that of infidelity. The essence of infidelity is the ultimate possibility that a new relationship will be formed and the marital relationship abandoned. The fear of losing a spouse to another is the characteristic of marital jealousy. Jealousy in all its forms is a triangular situation, in which the intimate relationship of two people is threatened by the intervention of a third.

According to Freud the most basic human triangular situation is that of parents and child. Given his instinctual basis of the growth of the personality, the rivalries are considered in sexual terms. The boy wishes to possess mother and exclude father and the girl to relate to father and exclude mother. The resolution of this Oedipus complex, as it is called, is thought to be fundamental in the development of the person. The rivalry can also be seen in terms of affection, namely that the child wants to have the exclusive attention of one parent and distance the other. Jealousy is also experienced when a younger baby arrives and competes for attention. Later on jealousy will be experienced in friendships, adolescent relationships and ultimately in marriage itself.

The persistence of marked jealousy in marriage indicates that the threat of loss of one's spouse to another is intimately linked with doubts and feelings of inferiority about one's own capacity to hold on to the partner. These feelings of inferiority may be social, intellectual, physical or emotional, but whatever their nature the jealous person is comparing themselves unfavourably with others who are constantly seen as potentially successful rivals.

A certain degree of jealousy is not uncommon and when a husband pays attention to another woman (or vice versa for the wife), it is accompanied by quarrels, sometimes bitter. These arguments are part of ordinary marital life and normally do not cause any permanent injury to it.

However, when a husband or wife knows that their partner is jealous, they can either reinforce this feeling by behaving in a flirtatious, provocative manner or they can try their hardest to reassure their insecure partner by acting with extreme care on all social occasions and avoiding giving rise to suspicion at other times. These precautions are ordinarily sufficient.

But in some people jealousy can be a marked trait, in which case the slightest gesture or sign, even looking at another man or woman, is interpreted as a betrayal. In these marriages the problems are more serious. The jealous husband or wife will try to restrict the freedom of their partner, question them unceasingly about their activities and even make false accusations.

Morbid jealousy

The marked forms of jealousy overlap with a condition which is clearly an illness and is called morbid jealousy. In this situation a spouse is convinced that their partner is having an affair and for this they produce evidence which is clearly delusional. By delusion psychiatrists mean a mistaken belief which is held tenaciously and is not open to reason.

The wife who is convinced that her husband is having an affair will interpret all his telephone calls as coming from the other woman, will examine his shirt for lipstick, his clothes for her hair, his underclothes for seminal stains and will undoubtedly find the 'evidence' where none exists. His visits will be monitored and his stays abroad checked. The extent of her suspicions and the need to verify them is unlimited, and the most minute detail will be interpreted according to her preconceived notions. None of his explanations will be believed and his refutations will be called lies. Such a woman is clearly mentally ill, and all the protestations of innocence on the part of her husband will not change the situation.

The same applies to the husband. He too may be deluded and be 'sure' that his wife is having an affair. Her movements, telephone calls, letters will be monitored and everything she does or says will be judged according to the conviction already held.

For such spouses suspicion is rampant, and if they can

afford it they will put detectives on the trail of their partner. They are constantly sure they have the proof that they want, but when examined in detail the so-called proof dissolves into a mere assortment of phantasies and circumstantial evidence.

Spouses who harbour this degree of suspicion will question their partner hour after hour and rarely be satisfied with the answers. The interrogation may continue into the early hours of the morning and the couple get progressively exhausted in the process.

There are a number of complications associated with morbid jealousy. The first is physical violence. At the height of the illness, the jealous partner may physically attack their spouse and, rarely, murder them. The second is the insistence that adultery has occurred and that the truth can only be arrived at by submitting the spouse to hypnosis or truth drugs. Thirdly, sometimes the accused partner admits to an affair for the sake of peace. But admission does not bring peace, it simply accentuates the questioning which asks for more and more detail of what happened. This incessant questioning for information applies to many jealous spouses, whether they are suffering from morbid jealousy or not. If their partner admits to any irregular behaviour, they become obsessed with the details and want to know how they compare with the rival.

Morbid jealousy is not easily amenable to marriage counselling and may need psychiatric intervention. Often the best that can be achieved is the agreement to continue to live together amicably but with the delusion ever present in the background.

Foul language

In the presence of sexual jealousy, the accuser may make liberal use of foul language. It is the husband who does this most frequently. He accuses his wife of looking and or behaving like a 'whore' or 'prostitute'. These names are used when the wife has done no more than talk to a man, have a dance with him, walk by his side or simply wear a dress that is seen as provocative. Wives are shocked when this abuse is first hurled at them. Husbands who use this language are not only jealous but may feel sexually inferior, and they project these feelings onto their wives who are seen as taunting them and behaving with a sexual freedom which is humiliating.

Counselling about jealousy

Counsellors of couples with these difficulties need first to help each partner recognize the anxiety and insecurity of the jealous spouse, which the other may be unaware of and accidentally reinforce. The next stage is to look at the origins of the jealous insecurity and to help the jealous person evaluate more carefully their resources and appreciate their positive aspects. Their partner needs to move from resentment and anger to an appreciation of their partner's fears of inadequacy, and to gradually reduce these by reassurance, praise and affirmation.

The more extreme forms may need psychiatric treatment including the use of anti-psychotic drugs.

Envy

Feelings of envy are often confused with jealousy but they are different. Envy is a feeling which concerns a comparison between two persons and is associated with the desire to possess what the other has. Envy starts very early in life, when a child feels inadequate and impoverished in relationship to mother or father. The parent appears to have everything and the child nothing. In this situation the child wants to be whatever the parent is. Later in life envy may lead to resentment, anger, violence and produce a competitive situation between spouses, in which one is trying to outbid the performance of the other. This leads to a lot of tension.

Once again the feelings of inadequacy and frustration have to be looked at carefully, and spouses have to appreciate the needs of each other. Provocation makes envious feelings worse, whereas these feelings abate with reassurance and praise.

Between them, jealousy and envy can make deep inroads into the harmony of a relationship. At their least destructive level such feelings lead to the desire to win arguments and be successful in all competitive situations between the spouses. Slightly more damaging is the subtle form of criticism about everything the spouse does, the imputation that they are proud and boastful and need constantly to be reduced to size. This criticism can become vicious, particularly on social occasions when spouses belittle each other mercilessly. Another form of subtle criticism is the use of jokes at each other's expense. In many of these exchanges envy is at the root of the problem, and since these are common complaints in marriage counselling they need careful attention.

Further reading

G. G. Clancton and L. Smith, *Jealousy.* Prentice-Hall, Englewood Cliffs, 1977.

M. Shepherd, 'Morbid Jealousy: Some Clinical and Social Aspects of a Psychiatric Symptom'. *(Journal of Mental Science,* 107, 687, 1961).

FIFTEEN

Sexual Variations

The title of this chapter may at first sight appear puzzling. Surely the topic is sexual deviations and not variations. The concept of deviation is linked with certain presuppositions which are deeply rooted in the Christian tradition. These are that sexual intercourse should result from heterosexual attraction, carried out in a penis-vagina penetration which is effected through a standard position of the wife lying under her husband. Any activity markedly different from this has been labelled a deviation in the past. The word deviation implies sexual and moral distortion, and any one interested in any different sexual approach was often thought to be abnormal. Clearly, if there is a basic conviction that all coitus should be linked with the possibility of the transmission of life, there are then fundamental moral issues involved in having intercourse outside the vagina, and in that case the beliefs of spouses enter into the discussion. But the vast majority of the issues do not concern fundamental moral values, only sexual habits disapproved of by society.

The recent rise of interest in sexual activity has spread to these matters, and increasingly an ideology is developing which accepts that what couples find pleasurable is also moral, provided that it is pursued with mutual consent. The various activities are now seen as variations and not deviations, and this introduces a measure of social and moral approbation.

The subjects to be considered here are not treated extensively, and they are only mentioned in the context of marital relations.

Homosexuality

Homosexuality is a part of the personality whereby sexual and often emotional attraction is directed towards a person of

similar sex. Homosexuality is a graded behaviour characteristic and can vary from an exclusive orientation to a
bisexual one. Clearly the exclusive homosexual is unlikely to
marry. Nevertheless problems can arise in the first phase of
marriage in a variety of ways. The homosexual person may
marry as a way of overcoming or treating their condition,
only to find that after a few acts of intercourse, sex with the
spouse becomes totally unacceptable and the relationship
comes to an end. The marriage may begin, only to find that
the homosexual spouse starts having extra-marital homosexual contacts which assume more significance than the
marriage. When a spouse knows that their partner is
homosexual, they can choose whether to proceed with the
marriage or not. The matter becomes a problem when the
homosexuality is concealed. In these circumstances the
outcome of the relationship depends on the response of the
partner, the presence of a strong affectionate bond, and that
of children.

But there is little doubt that some marriages come to an
abrupt end with the discovery that the partner's homosexuality makes normal sexual activity impossible.

Homosexuality may exist a long time in a marriage and be
discovered in the second phase, or its known presence may
become problematic during these years. This happens when
the homosexual partner finds they need an exclusive
homosexual relationship, which they achieve and they
suddenly leave home. More often the homosexual partner
may find themselves having an extra-marital affair which is
homosexual in nature, whilst trying to retain their marriage.
The affair may be serious or the extra-marital activity casual.
Thus a husband may be caught lingering in a public toilet or
become infected with venereal disease from a homosexual
prostitute contact. A wife may discover her husband's
orientation, for the first time, in this way. The wife may also
be having a lesbian affair which takes the husband completely
by surprise.

In all these circumstances it is necessary to assess two
things. First, does the homosexual partner wish the marriage
to continue and is homosexual activity a symptom of pressure
in their life. Thus a man may act out his homosexuality
because he is worried, depressed or is having marital

difficulties. The second issue is whether the homosexual spouse wishes to leave the marriage and establish a permanent relationship with another homosexual.

When the homosexual partner wishes to continue, the survival of the marriage depends on the ability of their spouse to live with the newly discovered situation. If affection is strong, the negative feelings may be overcome and the marriage continues. But if the marital relationship itself is under stress, the homosexual complication may be too much to bear. Sometimes the marriage continues with no further intercourse, but this depends on a compensatory presence of friendship and affection.

Finally such a marriage may continue until the children have grown up and then the partners separate, either to live alone or establish a separate homosexual relationship.

In summary a marriage between a homosexual and a heterosexual person can survive, particularly if the hetero-sexual partner knows and appreciates the situation and adapts to it. There may be strain if there is extra-marital homosexual activity, but this usually poses no threat to the marriage unless it is repeated or develops into a serious affair. When the partner does not know the orientation of their spouse and finds this out accidentally, the situation is more precarious. The outcome ultimately depends on the ability of the partner to tolerate it, which is more likely to happen if there is a good personal relationship.

Cross-dressing

The homosexual man and woman remains clearly identified with their gender. They do not wish to change sex. Rarely men and women want to change sex completely, and when this is effected the marriage is unlikely to survive.

More often one spouse, usually the husband, wants to dress in woman's clothes. This is a wish which may be revealed to their girl-friend prior to marriage and accepted. Sometimes the wife discovers her husband's secret after marriage. These desires may be very strong and sexual intercourse only possible when the man is dressed in feminine attire. What happens to such a relationship depends on the wife's attitude, which may vary from amused surprise to shock. In my experience cross-dressing, like so many variations, leads to marital difficulties only when the sexual and emotional dimensions deteriorate. Initially there is a good deal of tolerance by wives, who agree to participate in the variation and may even help their husbands with the cross-dressing.

Fetishes

A fetish is an object, usually unconnected with erotic significance, which has a specific sexual stimulation for the person concerned. Any object can become a fetish but usually soft, smooth material such as rubber, fur, silk are common ones. As with all sexual variations, fetish attraction is more common in husbands. They may want their wives to come to bed with a rubber coat, or lie on a rubber mat, wear fur or silk garments, the erotic arousal being sometimes associated with a specific colour such as black. Occasionally a man can only be aroused in the presence of a fetish and in its absence be totally impotent.

The desire for a fetish is much more common than is usually appreciated and many wives co-operate with their husbands. Difficulties arise when a wife feels that the fetish is becoming more important than herself, the object having replaced the person. Counselling in this situation requires the introduction of an awareness on the part of the husband that, however attractive the fetish is, intercourse is an activity between persons and, if he does not make his wife feel the focus of attention, she is likely to feel rejected and dismissed.

Sado-masochism

Sadism is the term used for the association of erotic pleasure with the infliction of pain and masochism the experience of erotic pleasure with the reception of pain. These desires are widespread, and at their most intense expression are linked with nauseating torture and human degradation. But in marriages one finds less marked manifestations, in which either partner wants to experience some mild pain or humiliation in order to be aroused erotically. The pages of the sexual magazines are littered with advertisements for sado-masochistic activities, and once again this is probably a far more common human activity than most people appreciate. The Freudian literature is full of reference to this topic, and there is little doubt that subtle and unconscious forms exist widely in marriage. Reference has been made to teasing, bullying and maltreatment throughout the pages of this book, and the remarkable thing is that spouses often tolerate this for long periods and sometimes for a lifetime. Not all tolerance is an expression of masochism; some partners accept such behaviour out of fear, emotional dependence and the absence of an alternative initiative. But on other occasions men and women appear to take some satisfaction from such treatment and indeed may provoke it.

In the more overt sado-masochistic situations a man may wish to be beaten or spanked by his wife, something which reminds him of similar events in childhood which were sexually exciting. Occasionally a husband wants to be tied or rendered helpless as the condition for maximum sexual excitation.

In all these situations wives and sometimes husbands may at first co-operate, later becoming reluctant to do so or refusing totally to have anything to do with it. In marital counselling these activities will sometimes emerge as the specific reason for the marital problem, but often it will be an addition to a long list of other complaints and will express most powerfully the feeling of being uncared for as a person.

Sexual orifices

Freudian theory suggests that the mouth and anus are sites of critical sexual development in the personality. Apart from the theoretical perspective both are orifices in which intercourse can take place. Wives may know of this predilection in their husband prior to marriage, or they may discover it afterwards. They may be excited by the idea, utterly shocked and/or have strong moral objections to these sites being used for coitus. Sometimes they may agree to experiment and then find it unacceptable, they may tolerate it without experiencing pleasure, or they may refuse totally.

Sometimes what happens in marital breakdown is that the

relationship deteriorates for other reasons and, when the solicitor asks for evidence, events which took place many years ago, when the wife was a willing partner, are given as a typical example of the husband's depravity. When a husband persists in pestering his wife with these desires and she is unwilling to oblige, then his conduct is clearly unacceptable and may be used against him. But when it was part of a loving experiment, it is unfair to rake it up and use it as part of the evidence. Husbands feel badly betrayed in these circumstances, and their desire to fight back may lead to an acrimonious divorce. Counselling may not prevent the divorce, but it may help to put the behaviour in perspective and avoid unnecessary pain and anger.

Conclusion

Marriage counselling needs to help a couple appreciate their social and moral values in these matters, so that one partner does not feel coerced to accept behaviour which is regarded as wrong or is experienced as disgusting. When the problem is not one of outraged social or moral feelings, the other objection is that the wife is treated as an object and not as a person in these activities, a situation which needs correcting.

Further reading

J. Bancroft, *Deviant Sexual Behaviour.* Oxford University Press, 1975.
P. Coleman, *Christian Attitudes to Homosexuality.* SPCK, 1980.
H. J. Eysenk, *Sex and Personality.* Open Books, 1976.
D. J. West, *Homosexuality Re-examined.* Duckworth, 1977.

SIXTEEN

Alcoholism

The presence of excessive alcohol intake can precipitate and/or aggravate marital problems, and this complication is common enough to warrant attention in its own right. The intrusion of alcohol abuse into marriage may occur in its early stages or more commonly in the second phase.

The first phase

In this stage heavy drinking, which can be daily, at week ends, periodic or occasional, is usually a pattern established before marriage. It is more common in men than women, although alcoholism has been increasing in the latter. Heavy drinking in these circumstances may be determined by cultural, family or personal reasons. The personal reasons are usually the presence of a combination of excessive anxiety and moodiness which is lifted by drink, at least temporarily. Excessive drinking may bring a marriage to an end in the first phase of marriage, if the spouse cannot cope with the problems it presents.

The second phase

In this phase heavy drinking and alcoholic dependence develop frequently for three reasons. The first is simply the continuation of the pattern in the first phase, heavy drinking gradually assuming the nature of an addiction. The second is the use of alcohol as a source of relief for non-marital problems at work, with money, relatives, following stress and personal unhappiness. Whilst the origin of this pattern may be unconnected with the marriage itself, it can certainly have an adverse impact on it. The third arises from the marriage itself. Marital conflict, unexpressed anger, unresolved tension arising from any of the problems discussed can lead to the resort to alcohol for relief.

The third phase

In this phase the pattern of alcoholism is either the continuation of life-long drinking, personal difficulties or unresolved marital problems.

Impact of alcohol on marriage

Heavy drinking usually occurs in the evening when a husband goes to the pub, in the company of friends or in the privacy of home.

When a man returns home drunk, several unpleasant events may happen. He may get into bed smelling of alcohol, totally unable to express loving feelings and attempt sexual intercourse. Excess consumption of alcohol may produce temporary impotence and he may be unable to make love, but the whole approach elicits a sense of disgust from his wife who finds it nauseating.

In the course of being drunk inhibitions are reduced, and the angry, frustrated spouse may treat their partner to lengthy abuse and, worse, physical violence, both of which are forgotten the next day except that the bruises remain. When both spouses are angry, alcohol can unleash a veritable blood-bath and some appalling scenes of violence. The children may observe these and may even feel obliged to protect their parent.

Apart from these excessive violations, drink makes a person unable to communicate properly. If they don't fall asleep, they are unattractive companions, so that they are no longer available to their spouse and children.

Finally there are the economic complications whereby families are left short of money and sometimes are financially destroyed through drink.

Management of alcoholic problems

When a spouse becomes physically and psychologically addicted to alcohol, there is little alternative other than to admit him/her to a unit to bring the excessive drinking under control. The alcoholic is drinking at all times, from the early hours of the morning to late evening. With this heavy drinking there is often a loss of appetite, an inability to concentrate, physical tremor, bouts of memory loss and possibly physical complications.

After admission to hospital and the treatment of the acute stage is completed, there is the long-term management. Despite various forms of therapy, no convincing solution has yet emerged which offers complete immunity to further drinking. Relapses are common.

As far as marriage-counselling is concerned, certain points are of vital importance. As with infidelity it is easy to make the alcoholic partner the scapegoat for the marital troubles. It is important to realize that alcohol is often a symptom, and that both partners need to examine their behaviour and appreciate what contribution they are making to the problem. The situation becomes complicated when one spouse has a predilection for drinking and this is accentuated by marital difficulties. There are however marriages where the problem really is that of one partner and the spouse has to live with it.

When the marital difficulties have been improved, the alcohol problem may disappear. When it remains, there are associations like the Alcoholics Anonymous which are helpful. When a spouse is trying to cope with their alcohol problem, the assistance and support of their partner is vital. Thus if a husband or wife attempts to stop drinking, their partner has to decide whether they will continue to drink and keep bottles in the house. The experts are still arguing whether total or partial abstention from drink is the answer for the rehabilitated alcoholic. Whatever course is advised, the spouse needs to be supportive and avoid provocation by any subtle encouragement of drinking.

Sometimes the continuous drinking of a spouse makes it impossible for their partner to stay with them. Occasionally the departing husband or wife may remain on friendly terms and be willing to return if drink is given up, a challenge which may be taken up and become the only motivation that changes the behaviour.

Conclusion

Alcoholic problems are often complex. Recovery is possible but it needs motivation, support from the spouse, release from worry and the resolution of marital problems. Marriage counselling can assist, when marital conflict exists, by clarifying the problems and showing that often both partners have a part to play.

Further reading

A. W. Clare, 'The Causes of Alcoholism', (*British Journal of Hospital Medicine,* 21,403, 1979).

J. Orford and J. Harwin, *Alcohol and the Family.* Croom Helm, 1982.

R. Smith, *Alcohol Problems.* British Medical Association, 1982.

SEVENTEEN

Violence

Any intimate relationship such as marriage is likely to mobilize love, anger and conflict. No family escapes from arguments, quarrels and even some severe conflict. This is to be expected and is usually negotiated by some exhibition of temper expressed in words, withdrawal and punishing behaviour. Nevertheless the majority of conflicts are resolved without too much damage to the continuing relationship.

This chapter deals with the next stage, when conflict is expressed in a violent form, sometimes verbally but more often than not physically. This violence ranges from a push to a blow and sometimes to severe physical damage. A good deal of the violence in society is to be found in the home. Reference has already been made to the presence of violence in association with alcoholism and morbid jealousy, but it may exist in its own right.

Origins of violence

There are three theories which account for human violence.

The first stems from the psychoanalytic theory of the personality in which aggression is considered a basic instinct. This is mobilized by itself or in association with sexuality, in a whole range of circumstances ranging from threats to survival to the frustration of love and sexuality.

The second theory makes no basic theoretical assumption about the presence of instincts. It is based on behaviouristic principles which imply that when a course of behaviour is frustrated then this leads to anger and ultimately to violence. Typical examples of such frustration are the unmet needs of food, sex and love, the rebuffs and rejections in personal encounters, and the threat of loss and actual loss such as those involved in jealousy and abandonment. The violent spouse often has a poor ability to cope with the slightest frustration.

The third is concerned with culture and environment. When a person grows up in a society which accepts violence as an appropriate response to frustration or in a home in which violence is used habitually, then simple learning and imitation accounts for its continuation.

There is much argument about the contribution that genetic factors make to aggressive behaviour. But the fact is that some adults, mostly men, who are aggressive, have had this characteristic from an early age or from adolescence, and this may suggest an inherited characteristic.

Finally it should be noted that the normal inhibitions to violent behaviour may be reduced when people are ill, depressed, anxious, paranoid or under the influence of drink or drugs.

Patterns of violence in marriage

In the first phase

The most likely exhibition of violence in this stage will come from a man or, much more rarely, from a woman who has a long history of aggression. When their history is taken in detail there will be previous incidents of physical violence against parents, casual acquaintances, friends and the police. These men react to the slightest frustration with a violent outburst, and their marriages do not survive for long.

Violence may also take place as an isolated event when conflict occurs. The violence may consist of a push, a blow or a slap across the face, repeated blows, seizing the wife by the hair and dragging her to the floor or kicking her. The conflict can arise from the problems mentioned in this phase, but the spouse is often someone with a low threshhold to frustration. This can escalate to actual murder attempts.

In the second phase

Violence in this phase is very often the result of change in a partner which is being blocked by their spouse. The wife who is angry and withdraws her affection or sexual availability, because she wants her independence and self assertion, is often the victim. Her constant refusal to accept 'common sense' as her husband would have it, the reiteration of her demands, interpreted as nagging, coupled with an unwilling-ness to have sex or to be nice to her husband, arouses extreme anger which spills over into violence.

Sometimes men slap their wives or simply take hold of them tightly to control what is interpreted as 'hysterical' behaviour. This behaviour consists of shouting and crying and is often an expression of desperation on the part of the wife, who feels that no other approach will make an impact. The husband sees her behaviour as that of a child in a temper and wants to control it. The wife is in a panic and the physical attack is the final act of outrage.

In the third phase
Violence may continue at this stage but it is less common.

Wife battering

In the last twenty years we have become conscious of physical violence towards wives which is persistent and severe and for which women's refuges have been set up. The question that is often asked is, why do wives tolerate such behaviour over a long time? The answers are complex. A psychoanalytic view is that women enjoy it in a masochistic way. It is possible that some women do, but the majority do not. Other factors operate.

Women who are battered may have grown up in an environment where violence was usual and they simply do not know any better. They are often married to men who have also grown up in violent families, and they too do not know how to behave in any other way. Frequently these women have nowhere to go and are anyway afraid of losing the little something they have in their home. When they try to leave, some husbands will simply not let them. They will pursue them wherever they go. These husbands are not only violent but also immature and dependent. They rely on their wife to an excessive degree and cannot cope without her. Instead of making it clear to her how much they need her, they try to terrorize her into submission.

Battering of children

As the battering of wives has now been recognized, so has that of children. Children of all ages are the recipients of the most persistent violence, causing physical injury, broken bones, burns and lacerations and scars which singly or collectively present a horrifying picture.

Research on battering mothers and fathers has revealed parents with a history of violence in their own upbringing, poor interpersonal relationship, little support by the husband and a woman who is often depressed, anxious and incompetent. The baby has also been shown to cry more, be restless and difficult to handle, leading to a combination of increasing frustration which is dealt with by physical violence.

Marriage counselling

The marriage counsellor has the task of helping a couple to acknowledge that physical violence does exist. Often it is denied by the husband, but, if he is reassured that no criticism or attack is going to be made on him, then he may feel sufficiently secure to admit it. A common-sense approach to marriage counselling may simply state that violence is unacceptable and leave it at that. But such 'advice' will not help. The counsellor has to assist the couple to recognize the problems which are leading to the conflict and whether in fact the normal control of the spouses is attenuated for any reason. Thus the counsellor has to help clarify both the reasons for the conflict and the aggravating circumstances. These may be alcohol, illness, stress or the sniping and flirtatious behaviour of the wife in social situations which leads to violence later at home. If the basic conflict cannot be resolved, then this may lead to separation or an agreement to avoid this particular area of provocation.

There are situations however when the violent spouse cannot change. In these circumstances counselling may be concerned with building up the confidence of the wife, so that she has the social and emotional ability to leave if this is what she wishes to do.

Needless to say that when a child is being battered then

action must be taken to protect it, and the Social Services Department or the NSPCC are the bodies responsible for intervention.

Further reading

R. E. Dobash and R. Dobash, *Violence against Wives.* Open Books, 1980.
J. J. Gayford, 'Wife Battering: a preliminary survey of 100 cases', (*British Medical Journal,* 1, 194, 1975).
J. Renvoize, *Web of Violence: A Study of Family Violence.* Routledge and Kegan Paul, 1978.
S. M. Smith and R. Harrison, '134 Battered Children: A medical and psychological study', (*British Journal of Medicine,* 3,666, 1974).
A. Storr, *Human Aggression.* Penguin, 1970.

EIGHTEEN

Depression

A depressive reaction is commonly associated with marital stress. A good deal of research has shown this connection. The problem with the word 'depression' is that it is used in different ways, covering a large area from a state of unhappiness to that of psychiatric illness. Whilst the former reaction is a natural concomitant of human distress, the latter is a severe change in mind and body which needs urgent medical attention.

Types of depression

If marriage counselling is to respond accurately to depression, it needs to appreciate the range and meaning of such reactions.

Depression is associated with mood change. Its feature is a change in mood from joy to sadness, from hope to misery, from well-being to pain and sometimes despair. Any adversity in life can bring about this reaction, which disappears spontaneously when the stress is removed.

This mood change may be associated with feelings of bodily discomfort, such as tension and anxiety, which in turn are linked with some disturbance of sleep. In this stage the depression has deepened and it involves the body as well, but it has not yet assumed the nature of illness. Such a reaction can still clear up spontaneously with the solution of the problem.

Finally a depressive mood may be accompanied by a wide range of physical and psychological symptoms. Physically such a person finds it difficult to sleep, loses their appetite and weight, has no sexual interest, cannot concentrate, feels lethargic, has poor memory, may feel weepy and ultimately despairing. The presence of these features suggests that depression has become an illness and needs medical intervention, because it will continue to persist even after the removal of the cause.

Suicidal behaviour

For over twenty-five years suicidal behaviour has been separated into suicidal attempts, called parasuicide, and suicide itself. In the former the person has no wish to die but makes a self-destructive gesture to draw attention to their plight. In the latter the intention is to terminate life. Suicidal attempts are intimately linked with marital problems and divorce. Tragically the gesture sometimes goes wrong and ends in death. Sometimes the spouse really wants to die, seeing this as the only way out of their predicament.

Depression and marital problems

There are three basic ways that depression and marriage are connected. The first is not immediately related to marital difficulties. A spouse may become depressed for reasons which are in no way connected with marital conflict. If the depression recurs frequently or is severe, it might begin to influence the marriage. The depressed person withdraws into himself and therefore becomes unavailable, loses their loving feelings, may lose interest in sex and radiates a sense of doom and gloom. This collapse of the personality can be a great strain on a marriage. If the depressed spouse is the wife, she gets up in the morning feeling dreadful, wants to do nothing, has no desire to go out shopping or visiting, is not interested in conversation and does not want to eat. She may gradually improve throughout the day and be at her best in the evening when her husband is nearly exhausted from the strain. So the presence of a depressed spouse day in day out, over weeks and months, may erode the marriage considerably.

The second reaction is the presence of a depressive reaction or illness which aggravates long-existent marital problems. When a spouse becomes depressed they lose their patience to be tolerant and understanding. Their capacity to cope with frustration becomes limited and they explode more frequently. They see their problems as if through a pair of dark spectacles which reinforces their gravity. Thus a combination of reduced ability to cope and a more gloomy perception of the problem may induce the desire to leave or end the marriage.

The third and commonest pattern is the triggering off of a depressive reaction or illness by the presence and persistence of a marital problem which appears insoluble. Mounting anger may be the cause of the depression or a sense of futility and despair that a spouse is not going to change or seek help. When spouses feel trapped, because they cannot see the possibility of change either in the marriage itself or through leaving it, they become depressed as a reaction to their sense of hopelessness, and it is in these circumstances that suicide gestures or suicide itself is made.

Post-puerperal depression

A very large number of women become depressed from a few hours to a few days after the birth of their child. A small number continue in this state for weeks, months and sometimes years. Accompanying the depression there may be loss of sexual feelings, irritability and chronic tiredness. These women feel worn out, and their marriages suffer a great deal. It is vital that a counsellor recognizes this state and asks for medical help for such a woman.

Marriage counselling

The marriage counsellor will often meet depressed clients. His task is to make some assessment of the degree of the depression, for if it is severe it needs referral to a medical agency. Otherwise it is the task of counselling to clarify and understand what is causing the depression and if possible to remedy this. The mere discussion of a problem can be extremely comforting and lift the mood, but on other occasions persistent counselling is needed to improve the depression. Some of this counselling is directed at improving the relationship of a couple who are both looking and working at the problem. On other occasions counselling is needed to assist the spouse, often the wife, whose husband refuses to co-operate. Such a woman needs help to see how she can cope with him, if she decides to stay, or gradually given the confidence to resolve the stalemate by leaving or confronting her husband.

Mention has often been made of the need to take into consideration the contribution of both spouses to a marital problem. This is particularly important, when one, who is often the wife, is depressed. It is only too easy in these circumstances to 'label' her as the sick person who only needs to get better. If the counsellor and/or doctor agrees with this formulation the wife is unlikely to get better, because her husband's contribution is not being recognized. Sometimes such a husband accuses his wife of being mentally ill, and in her depressed state such a woman may doubt her sanity or blame herself for what has gone wrong. On other occasions her husband threatens to send her to a mental hospital if she does not behave herself. Often the task of a counsellor is to reassure the wife that her mind is in good order, to recognize her depression and to link it with her legitimate complaint.

Another aspect of marriage counselling is the need to wait for the depression to lift in order to get a proper perspective of what the problem is. It may appear worse than it really is, and certainly it is important to ensure that no major decision about the future of the marriage is taken when a spouse is under the influence of depression.

Depression and marital breakdown

Depression is often triggered off by the experience of loss. In the last stages of marital difficulties, just before a couple split up or when a partner has left, depression is extremely common. It is of course at these moments that many people seek help. The depression experienced at these times can be very severe and also dangerous. Suicide is high in the interval between the breakdown of the marriage and the finding of a new intimate relationship, and anyone who threatens suicide at this juncture should be taken most seriously. People threaten suicide at various times in stormy marital situations and it is never easy to assess the seriousness of their intent.

Anyone who does voice such a feeling should be closely questioned about their intentions. If they really want to die, medical help should be sought without delay. If they wish they were dead but have no active intention of killing themselves there is less immediate threat, but when in doubt medical opinion should be sought.

When the depression is clearly linked with the loss of a spouse who is not likely to return and the condition has not reached illness severity and does not contain suicidal threats, then a counsellor has to remain available as long as the depressed person needs them. The sense of loss may take weeks, sometimes months and even years to be overcome. It is like a bereavement.

Management of depression

When a person is severely depressed, it is not appropriate to engage in marriage counselling. They need their depression treated with anti-depressants or even, occasionally, with electro-convulsive therapy (ECT). When the illness has lifted, then the stage of the marriage can be examined.

When the depression is not severe, it may still need anti-depressant therapy and counselling to be pursued simultaneously.

Depression with its manifold faces can be a confusing and complicating aspect of marriage counselling. The medically trained counsellor is likely to see a great deal more of it in practice, but everyone will encounter it and, when the lay counsellor is in doubt, getting a medical opinion is very helpful.

Further reading

J. Dominian, *Depression.* Fontana, 1981.
M. Hinchliffe *et al., The Melancholy Marriage.* Wiley, 1978.

PART FOUR

NINETEEN

Preventing Breakdown

Preparation for marriage

There is an increasing awareness that preparation for marriage is a necessity. Hopefully some preparation has taken place at home and at school, but that cannot be taken for granted. Some organizations like the Catholic Marriage Advisory Council have been running courses for engaged couples for over twenty years, and other denominations are also undertaking these.

Finally there is an opportunity for the minister who is going to marry them to do some constructive work with a couple prior to their marriage by having some sessions with them. In this chapter I want to concentrate on this opportunity that is available to the 60 per cent of first marriages which still take place in church. Each minister will evolve his own preparatory talk on the basis of his reading and experience. This chapter is not a substitute for such a conversation but a reminder of some salient points.

The contents for these sessions are taken from the world of research, and many of the points have been already alluded to in the book. My suggestion would be to have at least one session, preferably two and at the most three. These sessions should be used to consider the readiness and appropriateness of this particular marriage. The minister should not hesitate to say at the beginning that his task is to make the couple think about their preparedness to enter into marriage. One session, or part of a session, should be allocated to a separate interview for the man and woman and the rest to a combined one.

Separate interview
In this session the future spouse should be appraised of some clear links between courtship behaviour and the future

stability of the union. On reflection either partner may decide not to continue with the marriage or to postpone it or, being determined to proceed, it will be in the fuller knowledge of some of the risks involved.

The features that should be looked into in some detail are the presence of heavy drinking, gambling, promiscuous behaviour, excessive jealousy or violence.

Heavy drinking is a feature in a number of men and a minority of women. The danger is that at a later stage the drinking will become addictive with all the damage this implies. A man may shrug off warnings on the grounds that he can hold his drink, however extensive it may be, or that he can stop it at will. Every encouragement should be given to the girl to insist that he stops beforehand, and, if he cannot, he should avail himself of help. Future promises are not enough and the same applies to gambling.

As far as sexual behaviour is concerned, the man or woman who is unfaithful or promiscuous during courtship is likely to continue this behaviour after marriage. If their partner still wishes to marry them, they should do so with the knowledge of this possibility.

The same applies to the presence of marked jealousy. The jealous person is often unsure and insecure. They are constantly comparing themselves unfavourably with others and are worried about being displaced.

These people tend to be critical of themselves and of others. They are likely to be negative, make cutting remarks and be generally unpleasant. In addition to being jealous, critical and cynical, they are also likely to wish to restrict the freedom of their future spouse. When these characteristics are present, singly or in combination, they should act as a warning.

Care should also be taken with the presence of violence. If a man in particular has a low threshhold of frustration, is particularly sensitive to criticism and reacts to either with violent behaviour, then this is unlikely to change after marriage.

Either sex can be excessively sensitive to criticism and even misconstrue benign remarks as being derogatory. Such an attitude augurs ill for the relationship later on and should not be ignored, particularly if it is already distressing in the period of courtship.

Consent to marriage

Reference has already been made to the fact that when spouses talk about their problems later on, they often refer to the uncertainty, reluctance, marked doubt or even the sense of emotional compulsion with which they gave their consent to the marriage. It is imperative that the minister makes inquiries about the consent to marriage and the presence of any serious lingering doubt. If this exists, it should be explored and if necessary the marriage reconsidered. Too much stress cannot be placed on the need for real freedom in making the decision to marry.

Combined interview

Having explored singly the various factors mentioned, the couple should be seen together and be told that one of the main features of the change between courtship and marriage is the transition from falling in love to loving. Being in love is a state of heightened joy and pleasure in the presence of one's beloved. Good will is available in abundance, conflicts are forgiven and forgotten easily and a sense of variable bliss prevails.

After marriage the joy of the relationship will be found in the mutual sustaining, healing and growth of the various dimensions in the course of an unfolding relationship. The ecstasy will gradually disappear and a deeper experience of love will come about. Research findings suggest that the change takes place from the first day of marriage!

This drop in satisfaction will be felt even more when children arrive. There is a need to spell out the joy of having children and at the same time to point out that their presence dilutes the intimacy of the couple, reduces the available time together, increases fatigue for both partners and reduces, at least temporarily, sexual activity. All this should not be a warning against children but a preparation for their impact on the marriage. The other point that should also be mentioned is the need to recognize that both of them will change with the passage of time. When they see each other behave in new ways, some of them making demands on the relationship, they should recognize that this is a step in the right direction of mutual growth and should not be opposed.

In particular couples should anticipate that they will grow in their confidence, assertiveness, initiative and therefore in their demands on each other.

The couple should also be reminded of the inevitable presence of conflict in marriage. They have probably experienced arguments, quarrels, anger and reconciliation in their courtship. The same thing will happen in marriage. The specific point that needs to be mentioned is that, beyond forgiveness, there is the need for understanding the cause of repetitive behaviour. If a spouse continues with the same pattern of annoying behaviour the partner must try to help them understand why they are behaving in a particular way. Are there any clues in their childhood experiences, family life, culture or make-up of the personality, such as fear and anxiety? The need to try to understand a spouse and help them to change is of paramount importance.

Gender differences

The feminist movement would wish to claim that the sexes are exactly the same in all senses except the biological one of reproduction. This ideological approach makes sense in the light of a claimed superiority by men which is not remotely justified. As far as intelligence is concerned, there is ample evidence that the overall intelligence of the sexes in the same culture is the same. Nevertheless men tend to approach problems in terms of practical or rational solutions and women in terms of feelings, intuitive, social and personal answers.

These are generalizations, and individuals of both sexes can and do look at problems from the opposite sex's point of view. An awareness that both approaches are authentic should ensure that neither spouse dismisses the efforts of the other as irrelevant or wrong. The contrasts between reason and feeling, practical and social, concrete and personal, appear often in the way couples approach marital issues, and they should recognize this early on.

The other point that research is bringing to our attention is the fact that women recognize marital problems earlier than men, are often eager to do something about them and are more willing to talk about them to marriage counsellors. The lesson from these findings is that men should take far more seriously the early warnings of their wives and not dismiss them as nagging. Furthermore, when the wife suggests that a problem should be faced and talked through, this invitation should not be ignored. And ultimately, when she makes the suggestion that external help should be sought, the husband will be wise to agree.

Availability of a minister

The couple who are getting married may or may not stay in the parish of their marriage, but the minister should conclude these sessions by inviting the couple to drop him a card annually on their wedding anniversary to keep up a link between the onset of the sacrament and its continuation, and also to remind them that if they are in difficulties, wherever they are, they should contact him and see what assistance he can give to them. So often those in difficulties have no one to turn to, and this invitation ensures that there is one person to whom they can turn.

Conclusion

It is not expected that these sessions will eliminate marital breakdown. Their purpose is to stop any pending marriage which is clearly doomed and to give the couple a chance to think twice about any aspects of the relationship over which they feel unhappy. In addition, the information given in this chapter will help them to anticipate common problems, to recognize some of them earlier and, if the wife is taken seriously, to intervene effectively at an early phase of the marriage.

Further reading

M. Foley, *Preparing for Married Life*. Darton, Longman and Todd, 1981.

Preparing for Marriage. A folder published by the British Council of Churches' Division of Community Affairs, 1980.

Marriage between Anglicans and Roman Catholics. A pamphlet published by the Church Information Office and the Catholic Information Office, 1975.

Marriage Preparation

A practical programme of pre-marriage instructions containing 6 cassettes with accompanying written material for the minister and handouts for the couple. Produced by Redemptorist Publications, 1981.

TWENTY

Support for Marriage

Traditionally the task of the minister was to marry the couple in church. After the ceremony there was no formal concept of continuing pastoral care for marriage. Indeed the next time the couple were likely to be seen in church in connection with their family life was at the baptism of their child and later at its confirmation. Thus the wedding ceremony marked the culmination of the liturgical and pastoral involvement of the Church in marriage. This was the result of historical reasons which saw the wedding as the essence of the sacrament.

For the last thirty years, and particularly during the last decade, we have come to appreciate that the sacramental or holy nature of marriage lies in the relationship of the couple. Thus the wedding is the start of an unfolding relationship which extends over several decades, during which the life and love of the couple will be the basis of the marriage. It is abundantly clear that the Church has a crucial responsibility to support the couple during this period. So much of the emphasis hitherto has been directed at the care of the child. We now recognize that the well-being of children is directly related to that of their parents, and therefore the latter need to receive attention in their own right.

The supportive ministry must be concerned with the couple and not the wife and mother alone, although sometimes she will be needing her own special attention. The overall care for the couple is still a matter of experiment and innovation, and what follows are more illustrations of what is possible. What is important is that no parish should be without a plan for supporting marriage.

Support for the newly married

The newly married are likely to be assisted by their own families and friends. In some churches a habit is growing in which those marrying choose a couple who they invite to be their special friends, 'godparents' of sorts. Such a couple can remain available to help and be willing to discuss a wide range of matters but in particular to assist when there are personal problems which the newlyweds cannot work out for themselves or do not wish to involve their family. If both trust the couple, they can turn to them and, at the very least, talk about their problem. So many couples in difficulties find they have no one to confide in. It is important that the chosen couple are just a little older, have negotiated some of the hurdles of the early years of marriage, are unlikely to take sides in disputes and be willing to talk about the issues rather than give blunt advice.

Baptism and confirmation

Both baptism and confirmation are suitable occasions to have a session or more with the parents, not only to consider the meaning of these sacraments in the life of their child but also to consider the role of the parents as educators and in turn the importance of a good marital relationship which shows love as a model for the children to see and imitate. This is a good time to help parents appreciate the needs of their children in their development for personal love. But the growth of love in the children is closely linked with the married life of the couple, and it is a good time to reassess this.

Needs of parents after the advent of children

The arrival of a child is often associated with the cessation of work by the mother. The problem of lonely, isolated and sometimes depressed young mothers with nowhere to go and no one to see all day long has been recognized for some time. It is vital that every parish becomes familiar with the organizations available in the neighbourhood for young mothers in this predicament and that the mothers are encouraged in the right direction. If no facilities exist, then every effort should be made to start them, if possible on an ecumenical basis.

The young parents' time together is restricted with the

advent of a young child, and arrangements for baby-sitting can be immensely helpful. Again such arrangements often exist in the neighbourhood, and they should be known to the minister who will ensure that couples who need these services can find and make use of them.

Groups

A specific service to couples is the setting up of groups in a parish, or in combination with other parishes and preferably ecumenically, to discuss married and family life in its personal and spiritual dimensions. Groups of six couples, meeting monthly, can enrich the lives of the participants and gradually enable them to become the leaders of pastoral activity in the area.

Another alternative is to work with the local schools and examine the possibility of undertaking some programme for marriage. Mothers who come to collect their children from primary school can have a short meeting which is concerned with some aspects of family life. At all stages of the education of the child, the link between parenting and marriage can be a topic for consideration.

Liturgy

Apart from the wedding ceremony and the renewal of marriage vows there is no specific liturgy for marriage. In my book, *Marriage, Faith and Love,* I devote a chapter to this topic. I suggest there that we need an annual cycle of liturgy for the married. What I have in mind is that four Sundays, or weekdays, are chosen and a liturgy is prepared along denominational, or preferably ecumenical, lines in which the four phases of marriage, namely courtship, the early, middle and late years are focused by readings from the Old and the New Testaments, suitable prayers are constructed and an address is given by the minister or a lay person which is directed to the relational aspects of that particular phase. In this way couples can see their life experiences reflected in the liturgy and in return, through the liturgy, offer them to God. The need to spell out the contents of love in marriage and link them with the theology of marriage is an urgent necessity in the life of the nation.

Structures for support

If these developments are to take place, each diocese must have a committee concerned with married life. This committee should assist deaneries and parishes to have similar structures, so that every parish has a committee or suitable alternative unit concerned with marriage. I use the word 'marriage' rather than family because I want to focus on the couple. So often 'family' has meant in practice 'children', and the important message of this book is that the care of children depends on the stability and welfare of the parents.

Whenever possible ecumenical consultation and initiatives should take place, for this is a vital area of ecumenical work.

Research on marriage

The data on which this book has been based have largely come from research carried out on marriage in Britain and the United States in the last fifty years. An alliance between research, pastoral practice and support for marriage appears to be the ideal solution for the proper care of married people. Good research requires adequate funding, and I cannot think of an area in which the Church's resources have greater priority than in the understanding and advancement of marriage and the family. I look forward to the day when every parish will consider support of continuous work on marriage as part of its mission.

Conclusion

The support of marriage and the family has engaged our attention afresh in relation to the sudden rise of divorce. But divorce is a symptom of a more fundamental change in marriage itself, a change which is likely to spread from Western societies to the rest of the world. Thus in looking at the problems facing Western society in this area, we are witnessing basic issues which affect the man-woman relationship and the nature of being human which is ultimately a concern for everybody. Support for marriage is not only a matter of preventing marital breakdown but also the means of raising the level of experiencing love. For Christians there is a basic belief that whenever authentic love exists so does God, and for everyone the presence of love in marriage and the family is the most important way of realizing the fullness of being human. Love in the family is the most important bridge between man and God, and as such it deserves the highest priority we can give to it.

Index